Pulpit Poems

*For
Pastors And Bible Teachers,
Youth And Outreach Leaders,
Poetry Lovers & Daily Devotionals*

Written By Rev.
John Marinelli

Copyright

This book, "Pulpit Poems," is protected under the U.S. Copyright Laws. Rev. John Marinelli, author, copyrighted it in December of 2005 in Ocala, Florida. All rights are reserved except those granted here-in.

Copy Authorization

Authorization is given to reprint in any form as long as the author's name appears on the poem and it is not used for resale purposes. Feel free to use any poem for newsletters, bulletins, Bible studies, outreach ministries, etc. All other rights are reserved by the author.

Introduction

Pulpit Poems For Pastors And Bible Teachers was written over a 30-year period. It is a collection of anointed poetry that relates to specific Biblical stories, events and scripture passages. The poems are very suited as "Pulpit Poems" in conjunction with sermons, Sunday school lessons, newsletters and Bible studies.

The poems can also be used for posters, handouts; bulletin inserts and passes along ministry in nursing homes, prisons and Christian Fellowships.

The poems are presented in a random order to allow the Holy Spirit to minister on a variety of issues and theological topics. This offers the general reader repetition without boredom.

The table of contents makes this book the perfect pastoral reference and shows at lest three poems, if not more, on each of 54 doctrinal subject matters.

The author's objective is to share his God given gift with the body of Christ and to be a blessing to all who read his poetry.

About The Author
John Marinelli

Rev. Marinelli is an ordained Christian minister. John is the author of several other books, "The Art of Writing Christian Poetry", "Original Story Poems," a children's book, "Mysteries & Miracles," and "Moonlight & Mistletoe", which are Christian Fiction stories.

John has authored several one act plays and monologues that were marketed through Russell House Publishing to churches nationwide for use in their performance ministries. He is also a dedicated Christian poet with award winning poems, some of which are permanently displayed on 3' X 4'billboards in Holy Land USA, a 250 acre nature park in Bedford, VA. Several other poems are framed and displayed at the Christian Church Conference Center is Silver Springs, Florida.

He has appeared with his wife, Marilyn on several TV programs including "Bay Focus" in Tampa, Florida, Trinity Broadcasting Network in Jacksonville Beach and Miami, Florida, as well as, numerous radio station interviews around the country.

Table of Contents

| Category | Page Number |

Adoption
The Spirit of Adoption 32
In The Fullness of Time 9
The Pleasure of His Will 5

Angels
The Angels Cry Holy 36
My Guardian Angel 135
The Angel's Camp 138

Assurance
I Find My Self In God 13
"I AM" There 14
With Open Arms 123
It Came To Pass 41

Baptisms
Baptism By Fire 97
Baptism In The Holy Ghost 91
Baptism of Water 89
Spirit Baptism 191

Blood Atonement
Oh, The Blood 168
When He Sees The Blood 169
Blood Bought Redemption 163

Table of Contents

Chastisement
The Lord's Little 2 X 4 8
Train Up A Child..139
The Chastisement of the Lord..................................140

Christian Witness
Fragile Flower Red 57
God's Little Tree 88
The Glory of His Majesty 126

Christian Character
Godliness..68
As A Man Thinks, So Is He 141
The Perfect Man..136

Christmas
A Gift From The God of Eternity...............................86
Wise Men Still Seek Him 35
Shepherd's Field..37

Church
Peter And The Rock 46
A Glorious Church 67
The Gathering of Saints 186

Creation
Creation Groans 40
In Seven Days 137
God's Handiwork 142
All Creation Waits...3

Easter And The Cross
For The Joy Set Before Him 66
Easter Is..95
At The Cross 104
He Is Risen...93

Encouragement
A Mighty Refuge 207
Rest My Child 45
You're Going To Be Just Fine 133
The Lord Knows 100
The Lord Is 205
God Is Faithful 101
Stand Up Tall 122
The Master of The Sea 209

Faith
Faith 206
The Caveman's Prayer 65
The I Don't Know Scenario 74
Agreeing With God 1
Stinking Thinking 31
Is That All There Is 115

Fall of Man
One Man 172
The Passing of Death 173
God Said 174

Family
Little Children 80
A Husband's Manifesto 178
Submission 177

Father's Day
This Is My Father's Day 48
The Father's Promise 30
The Father's Glory 201

Fear And Doubt
Clutter 7
Faith And Fear 143
Overcoming Fear 145

Table of Contents

Fellowship With God
Galilee Oh Galilee 90
Rock of Ages 96
The Journey 22
Ask Me Know 103

Forgiveness
Beyond The Rainbow 52
Forgiveness 107
Forgive And Forget 147

Foreknowledge of God
The Was That Is 130
Before It Happens 148
From The Beginning 144

Free Will
Our Choice 175
The "Whosever Scenario" 42
The Invitation 176

Funerals
I Will Remember 116
The Sting of Death 200
Taste of Death 76

God, The Holy Trinity
One God 170
The Trinity 134
Almighty God 59

God's Love
From Tears To Smiles 58
The Master's Love 127
God Is Love 146

God's Wrath
Portrait of the Damned 117
After Grace...128
The Wrath of God 94

Grace
God's Grace 33
Grace Is Not A Magic Wand 180
Grace Defined 124

Healing
The Blind Man 28
Healing And Confession 125
By His Stripes 149
They Took Me To Jesus 48

Heaven
The Heavens Declare 16
Heaven Is His Throne 119
A Home In The Heavens...199

Hell
The Gates of Hell 47
Tongues of Hell's Fire 111
The Child of Hell 194

Holiness
A Highway Called," Holiness 38
To Be Holy 150
A Holy Priesthood...11
Holy Conversation 151

Holy Spirit
A Whisper In The Wind 51
Holy Spirit...112
The Comforter...152

Leadership
The Pastor And The Master 19
Blind Leaders 79

Intercession
Between Heaven And You 73
Our Intercessor 83
So Listen Up 15

Instruction
The Steps of A Good Man 129
Take Heed 153
A Word In Season 23

Judgments
Judgment of All Men 164
Judging Angels 183
Judging Secrets 82
The Judgment Seat of Christ 171
Obeying The Gospel 49

Justification
Grace That Justifies 179
God's Grace 33
The Justification of The Heathen 20

Marriage
Husbands And Wives 185
Two Become One 106
Male And Female 61

Mercy
All Paths 217
Mercy Endures Forever 108
Iniquity Purged 214

Obedience
Obedience Is Better 187
Obeying The Gospel 49
Obedience To Christ 113

Perseverance of the Saints
Tried By Fire 182
Help From Above 99
We Must Endure 109

Power of God
What Manor of Man Is This 132
A Mighty God Is He 154
The Sealing Power of God 155

Praise
The Power of Praise 78
Rejoice With Me 118
Praise Waits for Thee 156

Prayer
Our Time of Prayer 60
Prayer 81
All Creation Waits 3

Repentance
No One Should Perish 181
Except Ye Repent 75
Preaching Repentance 2

Resurrection
He Is Risen 93
The Stranger 212
Up From The Grave 204

Sacrifice

Types And Shadows	34
A Living Sacrifice	56
Propitiation	157

Salvation

Two Houses	55
There Is Still Time	62
Zacchaeus	211
Time Is Running Out	84
No Other Name	98
Two Thieves	24
The Lighthouse	25
Call Upon The Lord	39
A Well Not Made By Man	50
Consider The Clock	105
Portrait of The Damned	117
No One Should Perish	181
Except Ye Repent	75

Sin

Falling Short	193
One Man	172
An Offering For Sin	85

Social Issues

Thou Shalt Not Kill	(Abortion)	202
Gay Rights	(Homosexuality)	203
A Little Sleep	(Poverty)	195
Life Abundant	(Prosperity)	196
No Difference	(Racial Prejudice)	197
The Lion's Roar	(War)	198
Our Healer	(Healthcare)	213
God Will Take Care of Us	(Economy)	215

Spiritual Fruit
See O' Man 102
Flourishing 158
The Fruit of The Spirit 121

Spiritual Gifts
Gifts For All 110
The Best Gift 159
Neglected Gifts 71

Spiritual Growth
His Call To Glory 69
I Surrender All 114
Growing Pains 160

Spiritual Warfare
Winning The Battle 17
Little Prisons 44
The Wrestling Match 167

Stewardship
Stewards of Mysteries 10
Stewards of Grace 70
A Faithful And Wise Steward 192

Temptation
The Bread And The Stone 92
Arm's Length 6
A Way of Escape 161
Not By Bread Alone 208

Thanksgiving
I Love You Lord 53
Be Thankful 162
Thank You Heavenly Father 87

The Lord's Supper
The Broken Body 188
The Cup of Remembrance 189
The Unworthy Partaker...190

The Second Coming
A Glorious Church 67
He Is Coming Again..72
In The Twinkling of An Eye....................................12

Victory In Christ
Passing Over 54
With Eagle Wings 64
The Way Maker...27
The Power of Jesus' Name......................................43
Shout The Victory 120
Thy Soul To Keep 131

Word of God
A Lamp Unto My Feet 216
Quick And Powerful 26
The Hidden Word 21

Worry
Don't Worry 4
The Fretter...165
The Folly of Worry 166

Worship
Worship Is 184
True Worship...77
Worship In Holiness..18

Agreeing With God

We speak of things that are not,
Believing in them as though they were,
Because our Heavenly Father spoke them first,
Sending them to us in promises that never blur.

We take Him at His Word,
And listen to all He has to say.
We wrap each promise around our souls,
Until what was spoken becomes our day.

We will agree with the Lord,
Trusting that He knows best.
For only His awesome power,
Can provide our souls with rest.

"As it is written, I have made thee a father of many nations, before Him who he believed, even God who quickens the dead, and calls those things that be not as though they were" Romans 4:17

Like Abraham, we also have a destiny that God has spoken into our lives. He calls it forth before it exists. Like Abraham, we are to believe, even against hope, that what God said will indeed come to be. (Romans 4:18).

Let us hold fast to our belief and let our faith rest in the power of God's Word to accomplish what He sent it to do.

Preaching Repentance

But we preach repentance
For the remission of sin.
This we do in the name of Jesus,
That all men could know Him.

He is the joy of our lives
And the hope of our destiny.
This is what we preach
That all men should be free.

We are witnesses of these things,
For it indeed happened first to us.
We repented and believed on Him,
And now are free from sinful lusts.

"And that repentance and remission of sins should be preached in his name, among the nations, beginning at Jerusalem." Luke 24:7

We preach repentance because there is no salvation without it. We preach remission of sins because that is what happens when we repent. This we do among the nations as a witness of our faith and love for Jesus.

All Creation Waits

A blue-gray sky
Winks at the dawn,
As the morning light
Sings its glorious song.

Life is flourishing everywhere,
Unaware of what's in store.
The sounds of spring beckons,
In a silent and peaceful roar.

Time marches onward,
Towards the brink of day,
As all of creation waits
For God's children to pray.

"Finally Brethren, pray for us that the word of the Lord may have free course, and be glorified, even as it is with you: And that we may be delivered from unreasonable and wicked men, for all men have not faith." II Thessalonians 3:1 & 2

Prayer is where we commune with our Heavenly Father; where we talk to Jesus about life's trials, setbacks and future dreams. Prayer is where we fellowship with the Holy Spirit and are encouraged and strengthen for the journey ahead. Try it some time.

Don't Worry

Don't worry about tomorrow.
You did that yesterday.
Go on with your life
And remember always to pray.

Ask and it shall be given to you,
But this great truth you already know.
Rejoice and be happy, why? Because...
Your harvest comes from what you sow.

I will say it again and even more,
Until it becomes very very clear.
Tomorrow will take care of itself,
But worry is another word for fear.

Now here's what I want you to do.
Trust in the Lord and be of good cheer.
Drop the worry from your vocabulary
And cast out that demon of fear.

"Take therefore no thought for the morrow: for the morrow shall take thought for the things of itself. Sufficient unto the day is the evil thereof." Mathew 6:34

Remember that God is in control of the lives of those that are submitted to His love and care. His power is greater than anything.

Thinking about what we should wear, eat or do, in a worrisome way, is not good for us. It says that we do not trust Him or believe that He is really able to meet our needs.

Taking no thought is to rest in the Master's provision and love. Verse 33 of Matthew chapter six tells us how to accomplish this task. "But seek ye first the kingdom of God, and His righteousness, and all these things shall be added unto you"

The Pleasure of His Will

It is by the pleasure
Of God's good will,
That we were adopted,
His destiny to fulfill.

Predestined to be His children,
Before the world even began.
Called unto the Lord our God,
To enjoy the promise land.

Chosen by Jesus, the Christ,
We come to God this day,
To become His children,
By a new and living way.

"Even when we were dead in our sins, hath quickened us together with Christ. (By grace are ye saved.) Ephesians 1:5

God has called us out of sin and quickened us, or caused us to be made alive, that we should be His children. What a plan.

Arm's Length

I hold the world at arm's length,
That its choices do not interfere.
While it does its own thing,
I watch and wait over here.

My steps must not go that way,
For it's not where I need to be.
The Lord has shown me the path,
That will lead me to my destiny.

The call of the world is strong
And pulls at me now and then.
But I know that way
Is full of sorrow and sin.

I must move on in life
Beyond their beckoning call.
It's the right thing to do,
So I do not stumble or fall.

I will not be swayed or misled
By family, friends or business deal.
Their secret thoughts are not mine,
To consider, to admire or feel.

So I keep the world at "Arm's Length"
As I journey through this life.
My faith in Jesus keeps me strong,
As I walk in His glorious light.

"Love not the world, neither the things that are in the world. If any man loves the world, the love of the Father is not in him. For all that is in the world, the lust of the flesh, the lust of the eyes and the pride of life, is not of the Father, but of the world. And the world passes away and the lust thereof: But he that doeth the will of God abides forever. I John 2:15-17

It is more important to know God and to follow after Him, than to become entangled in life's lustful traps: for if we were to gain the whole world and lose our own soul, how terrible would that be?

Clutter

Clutter keeps the mind confused,
As images dance through the night.
Lost among those unimportant thoughts,
Are the dreams that once shinned bright.

An endless parade of fear and doubt,
Crowds the mind to destroy our day.
Ever soaring on the wings of the soul,
Until it has formed an evil array.

But clutter is by one's choice,
Of those who dance to its beat.
Better to face imaginations' due
Than to fall into utter defeat.

Be Quiet!!! Is our spirit's desperate cry,
As we call upon the name of the Lord.
Silence is our heart's desired prayer,
Until our minds are again restored.

"Keep thy heart with all diligence: for out of it are the issues of life" Proverbs 4:23

We make the final choices in life that either lead us astray or closer to the Lord. We chose what enters our hearts and fills our minds. May we always choose the path of righteousness and the way of peace.

The Lord's Little Two By Four

God has a little 2' X 4'
That rest on heaven's windowsill.
He uses it now and then,
When we stray from His will.

Sometimes we need a good "Bap";
With the Lord's little 2' X 4'
To knock out the confusion,
And help us to desire Him more.

The Lord's little 2' X 4'
Is what we sometimes need,
To get our thinking straight,
And keep our focus indeed.

The Lord's little 2' X 4'
Is fashioned from life's every trial,
So we do not stray from His will,
Or fall into an ungodly lifestyle.

"My son, despise not the chastening of the Lord; neither be weary of His correction: for whom the Lord loves, He corrects; even as a father his son, in whom he delights." Proverbs 3:11 & 12

It is a good thing to be corrected by God. We should not fear His rebuke for it is not His wrath, but rather a blessing from His love that keeps us moving on towards maturity.

In The Fullness of Time

In the fullness of time,
Jesus came, made of a woman.
Our Heavenly Father sent Him
Because our adoption was at hand.

He was born under the law,
So He might redeem us from it,
And to receive adoption as sons,
Being children of God, we sit.

We who God made His children,
Have the Spirit of His Son,
Deep within our heart of hearts,
So we can finally become one.

"But when the fullness of time was come, God sent forth his son, made of a woman, made under the law, to redeem them that were under the law, that we might receive the adoption of sons. And because we are sons, God has sent forth the spirit of his son into our hearts, crying, Abba, Father." Galatians 4:4-6

We are the adopted sons of God. We, like no other, have the indwelling presence of the Spirit of His Son, who cries out unto God the Father. If your spirit is not crying out to God, you may want to find out why?

Stewards of Mysteries

We are to give an account of ourselves,
As the stewards of the mysteries of God.
They are entrusted into our loving care,
That we may walk where angels trod.

To know the mysteries of His power,
His love, His salvation and all the rest.
This is a great honor to have and to hold.
That which God says is His very best.

So be that steward that you are called to be,
And manage that which is placed into your care.
God will ask for a reckoning one day soon,
And we shall account for all that was there.

"Let a man so account of us, as the ministers of Christ, and stewards of the mysteries of God." I Corinthians 4:1

If we are called to minister, as all Christians are, we are also asked to be stewards of the mysteries that the Lord reveals unto us, that the church may be edified.

A Holy Priesthood

We are called into a holy priesthood,
To serve the Lord with gladness.
We are His holy priests on earth,
To point the way so others find rest.

We are a nation of priest unto the Lord,
That seeks the salvation of a troubled world.
To represent Jesus to the families of the earth,
To every man and woman and boy and girl.

We are a chosen generation, called into service,
To share Jesus with those who do not know.
It is our joy to serve the Lord in gratitude.
His love and praises are ours to boldly show.

"Ye also, as lively stones, are built up a spiritual house, a holy priesthood, to offer up spiritual sacrifices, acceptable to God by Jesus Christ. But ye are a chosen generation, a royal priesthood, an holy nation, a peculiar people: that ye should show forth the praises of him who hath called you out of darkness into his marvelous light." I Peter 2:5 & 9

We are called to witness, intercede, preach, and to do the work of ministry to all who enter our world. That is a real eye opener. It's not just the church staff but it is all believers, led by the staff. Now we need to pray and fall in line as a holy priest, to our family, our church, and the world around us. It is high time to be about our Father's work and fulfill His calling.

In The Twinkle of An Eye

In the twinkle of an eye,
The Lord will come for me.
Before you can even blink,
I'll be with Jesus in eternity.

In the twinkle of an eye,
The trump of God will sound,
And all who love the Lord
Will be homeward bound.

In the twinkle of an eye,
The world will fall into despair.
When God's wrath is poured out,
On all who refuse to listen or care.

In the twinkle of an eye,
We shall shout the victory.
Spared from His judgment,
To complete our destiny.

In the twinkle of an eye,
Destine to come our way.
I long for that final blink,
When we all will shout, "Hurray"

"For the Lord Himself shall descend from heaven with a shout, with the voice of an archangel, and with the trump of God, and the dead in Christ shall rise first: then we which are alive and remain shall be caught up together with them in the clouds, to meet the Lord in the air: and so shall we ever be with the Lord" I Thessalonians 4: 16 & 17

The physical return of the Lord is a fact of scripture. We can count on it and draw strength from its reality. He will not leave us or forsake us. He has returned already through His Holy Spirit to guide us and bless us in every way. But, He will return in the flesh also, as He said He would, that all might see Him.

I Find Myself In God

I find myself in God.
He is my, "Everything"
I know that He is Lord,
My Life, My Hope, My King.

I find myself in God,
Not the ways of Sin.
Nor do I look to others,
To know who I really am.

I find myself in God,
To whom I bow on bended knee.
He alone is my joy and strength
And where I want to be.

"For we are His workmanship, created in Christ Jesus unto good works, which God hath before ordained, that we should walk in them" Ephesians 2:10

Knowing that we are created in Christ Jesus gives us confidence to walk in Christ, as He walked, along a pathway of good works. It is our joy and pleasure to be like Him. In Him we move and live and have our being.

"I AM" There

"I AM" There,
At the end of your broken dreams,
Before the sun rises over your day,
Prior to those tear-filled streams.

"I AM" There,
Down that road of despair,
When all appears to be lost,
And no one seems to care.

"I AM" There,
Over all of life's twists and turns,
When tomorrow is all but gone,
And when you are full of concerns.

"I AM" There,
Sayeth the Lord of Host,
To bring you hope and peace,
And the power of My Holy Ghost.

"I AM" There,
To be sure you make it through,
In the midst of every trial,
To bless your life and deliver you.

"I Am" There

"All power is given unto me in heaven and earth. Go ye therefore and teach all nations, baptizing them in the name of the Father, and of the Son, and of the Holy Ghost: Teaching them to observe all things, whatsoever I have commanded you: and lo, I am with you always, even unto the end of the world." Mathew 28:18-20

The Lord is with us always. He never leaves our side, even when we leave His. In every situation, He is there. It's time to count on His presence and trust in His care.

So Listen Up

I write this verse that all should know.
What I have to say is like a seed, ready to grow.
So listen up to all I have to say.
It could be the very blessing your heart needs today.

God has not given you a spirit of fear.
Instead, He has offered to dry up every tear.
He really loves you, even though you often fail.
His love and mercy follows you,
Enabling you to be the head and not the tail.

So do not worry or even fret.
That's why Jesus paid sin's awful debt.
Now go on in life to discover its victory
Knowing that Jesus has indeed set you free.

"For God hath not given us the spirit of fear: but of Power and of Love and a sound mine" II Timothy 1:7

There is nothing to fear except fear itself and that spirit has been defeated on the cross. We now have the Spirit of power and love and a sound mind. He will never leave us or forsake us. We are truly free.

The Heavens Declare

The heavens declare the glory of God,
And His handiwork is evident everywhere.
His love is seen in the sun and moon.
Even the stars shine forth with His care.

God is seen in all that we can see,
Even His invisible nature and God-Head.
He shows Himself in glorious light,
So all who desire Him can be led.

The glory of God and all that He will ever be,
Is revealed in the heavens each day and night.
So we can worship Him in Spirit and truth,
And follow Him all the days of our life.

"The heavens declare the glory of God; the firmament shows his handiwork. Day unto day utters speech, and night unto night shows knowledge." Psalm 19:1-2

Man is without excuse when it comes to knowing God. If there were any questions, as to the existence of God, the heavens declare His glory.

Winning The Battle

We must use the Word of God
To calm emotions that fray.
For the enemy never sleeps,
Until he has led us astray.

So when your emotions overflow
With feelings like depression and fear.
Know this! If you dwell in that place,
You invite the enemy to draw near.

When your emotions rage
With fiery darts aglow,
Stand in the power of the Lord,
Against its awful woe.

And if you get confused
And lost in the storm,
Put your thoughts on trial,
Rejecting all but heaven born.

You can win the battle
That rages within your soul.
By casting down imaginations,
And breaking Satan's hold.

Remember to focus on Jesus,
Holding the world at arm's length.
Lift up your head above the trial,
And the Lord will give you strength.

"For the weapons of our warfare are not carnal but mighty, through God, to the pulling down of strongholds: casting down imaginations and every high thing that exalts itself against the knowledge of God, and bringing into captivity every thought to the obedience of Christ." II Corinthians 10:3-5 The battle is in our minds and we win by putting our thoughts on trial and casting out all that oppose the knowledge of God. This is true victory.

Worship In Holiness

The beauty of holiness
The Spirit of the Lord.
Fills our spirits with love,
So our souls are restored.

We will worship the Lord
In the beauty of holiness.
Through all that life unfolds,
And will strive to enter His rest.

We will rest in the Lord's
Finished work of grace.
And the beauty of His holiness,
Will always set the pace.

"Give unto the Lord, the glory due his name; worship the Lord in the beauty of holiness." Psalm 29:2

In the beauty of holiness is the place where worship occurs. It is in that realm that we see God. There is no doubt that we cannot continue in sin and also worship the Lord. We must repent, turn from any hint of sin and seek the very face of God. This is true worship.

The Pastor & The Master

If the pastor doesn't follow the Master,
Then I cannot follow the pastor.
But if the pastor walks with the Master,
Then I can walk with the pastor.

When pastors stray from the Master,
The sheep will stray from the pastor.
But when the pastor loves the Master,
God blesses the sheep and the pastor.

Jesus is the pastor's Master,
And why the sheep follow the Pastor.
For He is Lord over the pastor.
That's why they call Him Master.

The pastor and the Master--
The Master and the pastor--
The sheep follow the pastor
When the pastor follows the Master.

"And to the angel of the church of the Laodiceans write: these thing says the Amen, the faithful and true witness, the beginning of the creation of God; I know your works, that they are neither cold or hot: I would that thou were cold or hot. So then because thou art luke-warm, and neither cold or hot, I will spew thee out of my mouth." Revelation 4:14-16

Pastors have a great responsibility to lead the flock of God. If they fail, many will fall prey to evil. However, the discerning heart will not follow a pastor that does not follow Jesus.

The Justification of The Heathen

God, foreseeing He would justify the heathen,
Spoke boldly unto the patriarch, Abraham.
He said that He would bless all nations,
Through faith in the blood of the Lamb.

We were once among the heathen,
And walked our own precarious way.
We could not have imagined,
That God would love us some day.

Yet He justified both great and small,
Through the cross of Calvary;
So those who would believe
Would, one day, walk in victory.

"And the scripture, foreseeing that God would justify the heathen through faith, preached, before the gospel, unto Abraham, saying, "in thee shall all nations be blessed." Galatians 3:8

God told Abraham a secret that would and could only happen through Jesus, down through the ages of time, yet already done in the heart of God.

The Hidden Word

I have hidden your Word, oh Lord,
Behind my heart's door.
That it will bless my soul,
During troubled times and more.

It is hidden in my heart,
As a guide to keep me sane.
The Word opens my eyes to truth,
As it sings your glorious refrain.

Here is where I commune with you,
In the pages of the written word.
I see your matchless love,
And soar like a graceful bird.

Your Word, oh Lord of glory,
Keeps me from committing sin.
Because it reveals your truth,
And changes my heart within.

"Thy word have I hid in my heart, that I may not sin against thee. "Psalm 119:10

The Word of God is our Bible. It is a lifeline to the knowledge of God. Knowing it and applying it keeps us from sinning against the love of God. This is the best reason I know to study, so we can show ourselves approved of God and kept by His truth.

The Journey

I am drawn into the wilderness,
By the hand of Almighty God.
Led by the Holy Ghost,
I watch for His gentle nod.

He beckons me to come,
Leaving all else behind,
That I may know Him,
In this moment of time.

Onward I journey
Towards an unknown land,
Ever seeking my Savior,
I come to Him as I am.

My soul seeks to worship
In the quiet hours of the day.
He asks of me to come closer,
So I will not fall or go astray.

My journey is to know Him,
Through every trial of life.
To walk by faith through grace,
Into His glorious light.

"And Moses said unto the people, remember this day, in which ye came out of Egypt, out of the house of bondage; for by strength of hand, the Lord brought you out from this place." Exodus 13:3

It is the hand of the Lord that delivers us and calls us unto Himself. Our hearts are strangely drawn to follow Him. He alone is our life and joy.

A Word In Season

I was wakened by the Lord
To hear as one who was educated.
He taught me day by day.
Every morning, His voice waited.

To speak a word in season
To those who are weary in heart.
This is what I now know to do,
Because God has set me apart.

A word at the time it is needed,
Is a blessing from the Lord.
That my tongue should speak
That which will surely restore.

Oh that God would continue,
To use my tongue in this way.
What a joy it is to speak in season,
That others would not go astray.

"The Lord God hath given me the tongue of the learned, that I should know how to speak a word in season to him that is weary: he wakeneth morning by morning, he wakeneth my ear to hear as the learned." Isaiah 50: 4

Pray that our Lord will use you and educate you to speak on His behalf to those that are weary. A word in season is a word just at the right time. When it imamates from the throne of God, it gives strength and comfort and peace to the tired saint.

Two Thieves

Two thieves separated
By the Son of Glory.
To the left and to the right,
They tell sins awful story.

One fights the cross
And hates the idea of death.
While the other acknowledges his sins
And seeks God's eternal rest.

The arrogant and the repentant
Die with their Redeemer.
As He pays sin's awful price,
Only one becomes a believer.

Here-in is a portrait
Of both pride and humility
Face to face with eternity,
Both will discover their destiny.

He who separates the two
Holds the power over death.
Both must die with Him
Yet only one finds eternal rest.

Which one are you?

"Then there were two thieves crucified with Him, one on the right hand and the other on the felt;" Mathew 27:38

Even at the point of death, we still have a choice. Why not decide today to follow Jesus instead of waiting until the last possible moment, when life is fading away and you are overwhelmed with stress. That's not the time to try to figure it out.

The Lighthouse

A lighthouse is a blessing,
To the ships that toss in the sea.
For it shows them the way,
Until they can clearly see.

The rage of an angry storm,
Cannot hide its brilliant light.
Nor can its awesome furry,
Rule as an endless night.

Jesus is the lighthouse,
For those who have gone astray.
The light of His love,
Offers a new and living way.

Jesus is the lighthouse,
When fear and sickness rage.
The light of His love,
Gives hope in difficult days.

So trust in the Lord,
And look for His light.
He alone is "The Lighthouse",
That guides you through the night.

"I am the Way, the Truth, and the Life. No man cometh to the Father but by me" John 14:6

Life holds many dark nights that are full of unexpected storms. Only a deep abiding faith in Jesus Christ will get us through. He is the light of the world. His light keeps us from falling into confusion, sorrow, sickness and demonic oppression.

Quick And Powerful

The Word of our God
Is quick and powerful.
It accomplishes all things
Whatsoever it is sent to do.

It is sure to cut asunder
The soul and the spirit,
And the joints and marrow,
So everything is brand new.

God's Word, the Bible
Is sharper than any sword.
It is able to cut away the sin,
That hinders us being restored.

Your Word, oh Lord
Judges the intent of the heart.
It is a discerner of thoughts.
And always keeps us apart.

"For the word of God is quick and powerful and sharper than any two-edged sword, piercing even to the dividing asunder of soul and spirit, and of joints and marrow, and is a discerner of the thoughts and intents of the heart." Hebrews 4:12

God's Word is all we need. Jesus said that man was supposed to live by every word that comes out of the mouth of God. It's high time to listen and live by His word. It will separate the flesh from the spirit, giving us freedom to serve God. All we have to do is let it happen.

The Way Maker

Only Jesus can make a way,
Through the difficulties of life.
He alone is Lord and King,
Over life's sorrows and strife.

He is the "Way Maker,"
When there is no visible way.
He will make the way known,
As though it were the light of day.

He will make a way,
For those of humble heart.
He will clear away the rubble,
Restoring what Satan broke apart.

Jesus is the "Way Maker,"
A friend to all who are lost.
He has made the way,
Paying sin's incredible cost.

The way to the Maker,
Is through His only Son.
He alone is the "Way Maker,"
Until life's battles are won.

"Let not your heart be troubled. Ye believe in God, believe also in me. In my father's house are many mansions: If it were not so, I would have told you. I go to prepare a place for you. And if I go and prepare a place for you, I will come again, and receive you unto myself, that where I am, there ye may be also." John 14: 1-3

The Lord is prepared for any emergency. He knows the beginning from the end and has gone before us to prepare a way that we can follow until we see Him face to face.

The Blind Man

I was blind from my birth,
Empty and alone on this earth,
Forced to walk by tap of staff,
Subject to people's love or wrath.

Day after endless day,
I sat in harms way,
Waiting for that jingle sound,
From beggar's cry to all around.

With people passing everywhere,
I only listened with empty stare,
Hoping for a generous soul,
To bless me with silver or gold.

As I begged from street to street,
By chance, a man, I happened to meet,
Jesus, the Christ, entered my day.
He brought love and peace my way.
He touched my eyes, with moistened clay,
Then told me to wash it all away.
Suddenly, I saw people looking at me.
It was a miracle, I could see.
But, when others heard, what Jesus had done,
They asked me, "where is this holy one?"
I could not show them the way,
So, they called the rulers of my day.

They asked me how I could see.
They wanted to know all about me.
But, when I told them of Jesus,
They were angry and caused a fuss.

The Blind Man (Continued)

They called my parents to speak up for me,
Saying, "How is it that your son can see?"
They said, "We do not know how or when.
Our son is of age, ask him."

So the rulers asked again of me,
Tell us now, How can you see?
I told them of Jesus once again,
But they continued to ridicule Him.

Finally, I spoke up loud,
Before the entire crowd
Saying, "Please, listen to me.
I once was blind but now I see."

They told me to leave and never return,
Rejecting the truth at every turn.
So I went on with my day,
Thankful that Jesus passed my way.

"And Jesus passed by and saw a man that was blind from his birth. And his disciples asked Him, saying Master, who did sin, this man or his parents, that he was born blind? Jesus answered, neither did this man sin nor his parents; but the works of God should be made manifest in him" John 9:1-3"

We are all born spiritually blind. We were blind in the heart but Jesus, passing our way, opened our blind eyes so we could see. This is the work of God that happens to every soul that believes in Him.

The Father's Promise

I tarried in the city of Jerusalem,
Waiting for the promise of the Father,
To be baptized with the Holy Ghost.

I knew that it wouldn't be long,
So I offered my prayers with others,
For the promise and God's utmost.

Suddenly, when all were in one accord,
A mighty rushing wind began to blow,
And tongues of fire filled the place.

We all spoke in other tongues,
To declare the glory of God,
And our language was of every race.

The Father's promise fell upon us all,
And changed the course of our destiny,
God and man, meet again, face to face.

"And being assembled together with them, commanded them that they should not depart from Jerusalem, but wait for the promise of the Father, which, sayeth he, ye have heard of me." Acts 1:4

The promise of the Father is the Holy Ghost and this promise is given to every generation. When He is come, He will speak of Jesus and endue the saints with power and special gifts so they can walk in victory under the same anointing that Jesus had while here on earth. This promise is none other than the reproduction of God in man, which is the original plan of God.

Stinking Thinking

Stinking thinking, they say,
Is bad for your health.
For it frustrates life's goals,
And denies happiness and wealth.

A right perspective is important,
As we think about everything.
It will either bring us down,
Or cause us to shout and sing.

What we think about these days,
Really does affect our life.
It can cause us to overflow with Joy,
Or fall into depression and strife.

So don't let your thinking,
Stink all the way up to heaven.
Stand in faith before God,
And get rid of that negative leaven.

"Then Jesus said unto them, Take heed and beware of the leaven of the Pharisees and the Sadducees" Mathew 16:6

Someone once said, "We are what we think" The Bible says, "As a man thinks, so is he" It is important to concentrate our thinking of those things that are of good report, pure, honest and that will keep us clean of heart.

The Spirit of Adoption

We did not receive
The spirit of bondage,
That would drag us back into fear.

Instead, we were blessed
With the spirit of adoption,
And now hold God's love near.

Herein we cry, Father
From spirit to Spirit,
In a new and living way.

Now His Holy Spirit
Bears witness with ours,
That we are His, forever to stay.

"For ye have not received the spirit of bondage again to fear, but ye have received the spirit of adoption, whereby we cry, Abba, Father." Romans 8: 15

There is a spirit of bondage and there is a Spirit of adoption. One spirit will drag you back into fear while the other adopts you into the family of God and teaches your hands to war so you can stay out of the traps of the devil. Which one have you received? Be honest.

God's Grace

God's grace is bestowed
Upon all who have sinned.
Freely given to justify all.

We are justified
By His wonderful grace
That we may receive Him.

He alone is our Savior,
And by His grace
We are free from sin.

Just-As-If-I'd
Never ever sinned
Is what grace means to me.

It is unmerited favor.
A gift of endless love
From the God of eternity.

"For all have sinned and come short of the glory of God. Being justified freely by his grace, through the redemption that is in Christ Jesus." Romans 3:23-24

Grace is, "Just-As-If-I'd" never ever sinned and God has placed all believers into this status. Of course, to be a believer, is to demonstrate personal faith in Jesus as your savior.

Types And Shadows

Types and Shadows,
Are all around.
In Abraham and Isaac,
They are surely found.

Isaac, a willing participant,
At the hands of his father's knife.
A test of love and obedience,
A shadow of salvation's light.

Obedient to his father,
Ready to offer up his soul.
Isaac, lay upon the alter,
So the Bible story is told.

Yet Isaac's life was spared,
As God provided another sacrifice.
He was only a Type and a Shadow.
Of Jesus, who paid sin's awful price.

"And He said, take now thy son, thine only son, Isaac, whom thou love, and get the into the land of Moriah, and offer him there for a burnt offering upon one of the mountains which I will tell thee of." Genesis 22: 2

Jesus was pictured in the Old Testament that we might realize the greatness of the gospel story; that was told in shadows and images long before it became a clear revelation.

Wise Men Still Seek Him

Wise men still seek Him
Who appeared so long ago.
They come now by grace
Through faithful hearts aglow.

Wise men still seek Him
For He is their "Bread of Life."
A sustaining inner strength
Through times of sorrow or strife.

Wise men still seek Him
The Christ of Calvary.
God's only begotten Son
Crucified as Sin's penalty.

Wise men still seek Him
Jesus, God in human array.
King of kings & Lord of lords
Born to earth on Christmas Day.

"Now when Jesus was born in Bethlehem of Judea in the days of Herod the king, behold, there came wise men from the east to Jerusalem, saying, where is he that is born king of the Jews? For we have seen his star in the east and are come to worship him" Mathew 2:1-2

Seeking Jesus is the wisest thing any man, woman or child can do and when we find Him, it is our privilege to bow down and worship Him. This is our journey, our destiny and our life while on this earth.

The Angels Cry Holy

The Angels cry "Holy,"
While sorrow fills the land.
For God's Judgment Day,
Is to come upon every man.

The Angels cry "Holy,"
While mankind goes astray,
Rejecting the love of God,
To follow his own precarious way.

The Angels cry "Holy,"
Knowing the terror of the Lord,
When all who dwell in sin,
Will suddenly be destroyed.

The Angels cry "Holy,"
Waiting for all things new,
Born of the Holy Spirit,
When God's Judgment is through.

The Angels cry "Holy,"
"Holy is the Lamb,"
Waiting for the children of God,
To join "The Great I AM"

"And one cried unto another and said, "Holy, Holy, Holy, is the Lord of host: the whole earth is full of his glory" Isaiah 6:3

We serve a Holy God that deserves our reverence and homage. The angels know this and worship Him, but man, because of sin, has no real concept of his own creator.

Shepherd's Field

God didn't choose the house of a king
To announce our Lord's birth that day.
Instead, He chose a shepherd's field,
And sent a might angel their way.

The shepherds were tending sheep,
That glorious and wonderful night.
It was just another task to be done,
Until they saw the angel by starlight.

Upon their faces they fell,
As more angels appeared in the sky.
It was though time stopped,
As all the angels drew nigh.

But fear gave way to great joy,
As the angels began to sing.
Jesus, the Christ, is born this day,
Our Lord! Our Savior! Our King.

"And there were in the same country shepherds abiding in the field, keeping watch over their flock by night, and lo, the angel of the Lord came upon them and the glory of the Lord shone around about them: and they were sore afraid: And the angel said unto them, Fear not: for behold, I bring you good tidings of great joy, which shall be to all people. For unto you is born this day in the city of David, a savior, which is Christ, the Lord" Luke 2:8-11

Aren't you glad that the angel said that the "Good Tidings of great joy" was for all people? That means all people, not a select few or a super race. Jesus is for all of us to love and cherish.

A Highway Called "Holiness"

He places my feet on
A highway called "Holiness,"
That led my soul
To the throne of God.

Amidst the cheers of angels,
I walk, wearing His holy gown.
Onward towards heaven's throne,
While evil cast its awful frown.

My eyes were opened
That I might see.
Both the good and the evil,
That sought after me.

I walk the highway-Holiness
That crosses all of time.
Towards the throne of God,
Leaving this world behind.

"And an highway shall be there, and a way, and it shall be called, the way of holiness; the unclean shall not pass over it; but it shall be for those: the wayfaring men, though fools, shall not err therein. No lion shall be there, nor any ravenous beast shall go up thereon, it shall not be found there, but the redeemed shall walk there. And the redeemed of the Lord shall return, and come to Zion with songs and everlasting joy upon their heads: They shall obtain joy and gladness, and sorrow and sighing shall flee away." Isaiah 35:8-10

What a privilege to walk the highway of Holiness. It is prepared especially for us, the redeemed, and it is protected from the errors of fools and the snarl of beast and especially the roar of the lion.

Call Upon The Lord

When your burdens overwhelm you,
Like a mighty raging sea.
Call upon the Lord, Jesus,
And He will set you free

When your heartaches are many,
And life is difficult to understand.
Call upon the Lord, Jesus.
He will come and hold your hand.

When your friends reject you,
Because you follow after Him,
Call upon the Lord, Jesus.
And keep yourself from sin.

When you fall into depression,
As though it were a giant pit.
Call upon the Lord, Jesus,
Who will restore your joyful wit.

When you're saddened by the day
Feeling lost and all alone.
Call upon the Lord, Jesus,
Who will make His way known.

When you are weary and heavy laden,
Tired from life's many tests.
Call upon the Lord, Jesus,
Who is sure to give you rest.

"Hear my cry; oh God, attend unto my prayer. From the end of the earth, I will cry unto thee, when my heart is overwhelmed: Lead me to the rock that is higher than I." Psalms 61:1-2

Calling upon the Lord in stressful times is o.k. He wants us to cry to Him and then to trust in Him to watch over His Word to perform it on our behalf.

Creation Groans

The creatures' expectations
Shall all come true.
Their earnest desire
Is to see what God will do.

With groaning and longing,
From deep within,
The creatures wait,
For deliverance from sin.

Subjected to vanity
By the powers to be.
They too shall be delivered,
Through the cross of Calvary.

With expectations of love,
All of creation groans inside,
Waiting for the sons of God,
So they can dwell by their side

"For the earnest expectation of the creature waits for the manifestation of the sons of God. For the creature was made subject to vanity, not willingly, but be reason of him who has subjected the same in hope, because the creature itself shall also be delivered from the bondage of corruption into the glorious liberty of the children of God" Romans 8:19-21

Man has a responsibility to care for the animals, knowing they are subjected to his own vanity. They await the manifestation of the sons of God so they can get the proper care and love God wanted them to have. Be sure that you are treating your pets with love and respect.

It Came To Pass

Things often come to pass,
But seldom do they ever last.
They come into our busy day,
For awhile, then pass away.

We hear their voices, loud and clear,
As they arrive and while they are here.
They speak both joy and misery,
Some to you and some to me.

We say, "It came to pass,"
Or say, "It happened so fast."
Down life's beaten path,
Comes both love and wrath.

So say goodbye to sad and blue.
To all that is now troubling you.
For things will come, only to pass,
But God's love will always last.

"And it came to pass in those days…" Luke2:1

These are the times of our lives. We live them, some for good and some for not so good. One thing is for sure, that which comes our way, comes only to pass on by. It is not what happens that is so important, but rather what we do with what we are faced with.

Trusting in the Lord and seeking His guidance will always conquer that which comes to pass.

The Whosoever Scenario

The "Whosoever" is who so ever,
Not who so won't, can't or will not.
The story is as clear as a sunny day.
God offers a new and living way.

But only those who engage "free will"
To choose life, faith and obedience,
Will find salvation for their souls,
And be cleansed and made whole.

We do the choosing: to accept or deny.
That is how God set it up to be.
He made the call to life's "Whosoever",
That they could have live abundantly.

"For God so loved the world, that he gave his only begotten son, that whosoever believeth in him, should not perish but have everlasting life." John 3:16

We are the "Whosoever" in John 3:16, that one day put his or her faith in Christ, believed in Him and now rest in the Lord's love and grace. We have the promise of God that He sent His Son so we could believe and have everlasting life. How great is that?

The Power of Jesus' Name

The power of Jesus' Holy name
Has healed the sick and cured the lame.
It's opened the eyes of those once blind,
And sets men free, time after time.

The power of Jesus' matchless name
Was born through suffering and shame.
When Jesus fought for the souls of men
And gained the victory over every sin.

The power of Jesus' glorious name,
Is God's gift for all to claim.
Free for the asking and given in love,
To all who believe in God above.

Yes, there is power in Jesus' name.
That's the reason He came,
To free us from our every sin
And bring our hearts back to Him.

"That at the name of Jesus every knee should bow, of things in heaven, and things in earth and things under the earth, and that every tongue should confess that Jesus Christ, is Lord, to the glory of the Father" Philippians 2:10-11

Use the name of Jesus to fight against demons, against the carnality of the flesh and against evil communications. His name is full of power and majesty. It will keep you.

Little Prisons

Little prisons await the man with a lustful soul.
Bars of selfishness and pride create dungeons of icy cold.

Prisons of shame and jealousy fill the heart with utter despair.
Bars that separate from God and those that really care.

Stand back! While the doors are tightly closed;
Taking away your life, to wither as a dying rose.

Beware of those little prisons that trap the lustful soul.
Keep yourself free from sin through faith in the Christ of old.

Little prisons need not to be your fate.
It is your choice, Spirit or flesh to date.

"O Foolish Galatians, who hath bewitched you, that ye should not obey the truth, before whose eyes Jesus Christ hath been, evidently set forth, crucified among you? Are you so foolish? Having begun in the Spirit, are you now made perfect in the flesh?

We should always seek to dwell in the Spirit, that we would not emulate the deeds of the flesh. When we fall short, we create "little prisons" that keep us in confusion and away from the blessing of God. It's time to walk in the Spirit and break the prisons that so easily beset us.

Rest My Child

Rest my child, sayeth the Lord.
Take thy peace and be restored.
I have provided, thy mouth to feed.
From the beginning, I knew your need.

Do not worry, fret or even fear,
for, my child, I am always near.
To bless thy soul with love and grace,
To be with thee, face to face.

Come, my child, near to my throne.
Do not allow your faith to roam.
For those who will not believe,
Can never find rest in times of need.

My word shall see you through.
My grace I freely give to you.
That you should rest, thy soul to keep,
Forever delivered from unbelief

"And straightway the father of the child cried out, and said with tears, Lord, I believe, help my unbelief" Mark 9:24

When we believe God's Word, we find rest. When we don't, we fall into unbelief where there is no rest. Let us rest in the finished work of grace and rejoice in the day that God has made.

Peter & The Rock

Peter is not the rock of ages,
That Jesus built His church upon.
For he was only one of twelve,
That fought the devil and won.

The rock that the church is upon
Is the anointing Jesus walked in;
The power of the Holy Ghost.
That's what caused Him to win.

The gates of hell cannot overcome,
The anointing of Christ, our Lord.
For it is the power of almighty God,
Able to heal, to save and to restore.

Jesus is the Rock of Ages;
The builder and cornerstone,
Of a glorious and living church,
Without spot or wrinkled bone.

And Simon Peter answered and said, thou art the Christ, the son of the living God. Blessed art thou Simon Bar-jona: for flesh and blood hath not revealed it unto the, but my Father which is in heaven. And I say also unto thee, thou art Peter, and upon this rock, I will build my church; and the gates of hell shall not prevail against it." Mathew 16:16-18

Peter is a small rock. But, the Rock of the church is revealed in verse 16. It is the revelation that Peter had, that showed the true identity of Jesus. He is the Anointed One, The Christ.

The Gates of Hell

The gates of hell are not pearly white
And full of laughter, love or singing.
Instead, they are ablaze with sorrow and pain
And life has no purpose or real meaning.

A place of torment and suffering for evils' due.
That's what hell will be for all who enter therein.
Yet its gates will not prevail against the church.
Nor will its fury, sorrow and sin ever win.

The church will prevail over hell and death
Because Jesus now has its keys.
He is the victor over hell and the grave
And why we, in worship, fall to our knees.

"And I say unto the, thou art Peter, and upon this rock, I will build my church; and the gates of hell shall not prevail against it." Mathew 16:19

The economy of hell, with all its alluring images, shall never prevail or overcome the church, for she is the bride of Christ, a chased virgin in spirit without spot or wrinkle.

This Is My Father's Day

This is my Father's day,
Who formed the stars above
And washed my sins away
With the power of His love.

This is my Father's day,
Whose Son died for me.
When I was far, far away,
He came to set me free.

This is my Father's day
Who chose to call me, Son.
He taught me how to pray,
And caused my enemies to run.

This is my Father's day
To whom my hands I raise.
In life and peaceful array,
My Father God I praise.

"Behold, what manor of love hath the Father shown towards us, that we should be called the sons of God" I John 3:1

A true celebration of Father's Day is to rejoice and be glad that this is our Father's day that which is in heaven, because He has redeemed us and loves us.

Obeying The Gospel

Rest oh weary saint
That honors the Lord on High.
You who hold fast to the gospel
And refuse to believe the lie.

The time shall surely come
And is even now is at hand,
When Jesus will be revealed,
To judge the lives of every man.

As a flame of burning fire,
The Lord will surely shine.
But those that reject the gospel,
Will be lost in hell, for all of time.

"And to you who are troubled, rest with us, when the Lord Jesus shall be revealed from heaven with his mighty angels, in flaming fire, taking vengeance on them that know not God, and that obey not the gospel of our Lord Jesus Christ." I Thessalonians 1:7-8

We who serve the Lord and respect Him and honor the gospel can rest with all saints, knowing that Jesus will soon be revealed and He is coming with vengeance towards those who laugh at you and the gospel you obey.

A Well Not Made By Man

Wells that are made with human hands,
Draw the thirsty only to drink again.
The well is never deep enough
To quench the thirsty souls of men.

But there is a well, not made by man,
Whose water runs deep and pure.
Endlessly flowing with God's love,
It satisfies our thirst for more.

Come to the well, not made by man,
That you may drink your fill.
The Lord will give you to drink,
In accordance with His will.

Jesus is the Well, not made by man,
For all who thirst along life's way.
He is our well of "Living Water",
Sent by God to refresh our day.

"But whosoever shall drink of the water that I shall give him, shall never thirst; but the water that I shall give him, shall be in him a well of water, springing up into everlasting life" John 4: 14

A well of water, inside of us, that springs up into everlasting life. This is living water that continually flows for our refreshment, nourishment and health. This is the essence of eternal life.

A Whisper in the Wind

There's a whisper in the wind
That lingers both day and night.
A champion of truth and justice,
By the power of His might.

A word in due season
That echoes from deep within.
A voice out of nowhere,
Reproving the world of sin.

Look there, in the street
And here, by the shores of the sea.
There's a whisper hidden in the wind;
A voice from eternity.

There's a calling from God.
His voice is hidden in the wind.
In a whisper, He speaks to our hearts
With the love and counsel of a friend.

Listen for the Whisper,
All who seek to know.
It is God's Holy Spirit
Telling you which way to go.

"And thine ears shall hear a word behind thee saying, This is the way, walk ye in it, when ye turn to the right hand and when ye turn to the left" Isaiah 30:21

The voice of the Lord is often a still small voice, yet always clear and it never brings confusion. His voice is like a whisper in the wind that brings a peaceful breeze to the heart. The joy of hearing His voice is to know His will and our destiny.

Beyond The Rainbow

I traveled beyond the rainbow
To see all that I could see.
I gazed at the beauty of the stars
And looked into the door of eternity.

But when I stood up,
To see if there was more,
I saw the face of Love,
Smiling, as if to adore.

No words were ever spoken
And yet I heard an awesome cry.
A voice that said, "I love you,"
As His shadow drew nigh.

Joy raced around my head
And peace flowed within my soul.
I began to weep and laugh, and shout,
As His presence melted away the cold.

Finally I found forgiveness
From a long and sinful life.
The love of God set me free
From all pain and inward strife.

Glory be to God and Jesus,
His only begotten Son.
He alone holds my future
And declares that I have won.

"Then Jesus said to those Jews that believed on Him; If ye continue in my word, then ye are my disciples indeed: And ye shall know the truth and the truth shall make you free" John 8:31 & 32

True freedom comes when we encounter Jesus and believe on Him. It is then and only then that we find forgiveness, peace and any hope of life eternal.

I Love You Lord

I love You Lord
Because You first loved me.
I was bound by sin
Until Your love set me free.

I love You Lord,
Because now I can see.
I was once blind
Until Your love healed me.

I love You Lord
Because You are my victory.
I was afraid and alone
Until Your love comforted me.

I love you Lord
Because You are my stability.
I stumbled through life
Until Your love strengthened me.

I love You Lord
Because of Mount Calvary.
I was lost and without hope
Until Your love found me.

I love you Lord

"Herein is love, not that we loved God, But that He loved us, and sent His Son to be the propitiation for our sins" I John 4:10

We love Him because He first loved us. He initiated contact, showered us with blessings, showed us the way, and even now continues to encourage us and guide us to Himself. That's why we love Him.

Passing Over

"Let us pass over unto the other side",
Said Jesus, at the Sea of Galilee.
His faith rested in His father's will
And that He had a divine destiny.

No wind or storm held the power
To change His faith into fear.
He rested in His Father's word
As His fearful disciples drew near.

But if we, Like Jesus,
Could keep our eyes on God's will,
No storm that comes our way
Can say to our faith, "Be Still."

"And the same day, when even was come, He said unto them, Let us pass over unto the other side" Mark 4:35 (Full story 4:1-.41)

During the journey of life, we will encounter storms. But, God's will, as spoken in His Word, is sure to calm every storm because it carries the power of Jesus' name and the divine destiny of God.

Two Houses

We built our homes together,
Mine upon a Rock and his in the sand.
He thought his would be all right,
But he was a foolish man.

God's wisdom showed me the way
And what I needed to do.
But my foolish neighbor,
Never had a clue.

Then the rains came
And the winds began to blow.
The storms beat upon our homes
And we had nowhere to go.

We built our homes together,
My neighbor and me.
Mine is still there upon the Rock,
But his ceased to be.

Wise men and fools both suffer
The storms that befall mankind.
But those who trust in Jesus
Will always stand the test of time.

"Therefore whosoever hears these sayings of mine, and doeth them, I will liken him unto a wise man, which built his house upon a rock" Mathew 7: 24 (Story thru v-27)

There are always two paths to walk, two roads to follow, and two choices in life for every decision. The choice we make could very well be the destruction of our home, family and lifestyle. To be like the wise man, we must decide to follow Jesus and build our existence and future on Him.

A Living Sacrifice

We are to present ourselves to God
As a living sacrifice,
So the things of the flesh
Will dissolve like melting ice.

This is our service to the Lord,
A reasonable thing to do,
Seeing He became a sacrifice
So we could make it through.

Life with Jesus is more important
Than us dwelling in the flesh.
God wants us to be free
And enter into His eternal rest.

We are, as He is towards us,
A living sacrifice today,
That we could be like Him,
To walk in the Spirit every day.

"I beseech you therefore, brethren, by the mercies of God, that you present your bodies a living sacrifice, holy, acceptable unto God, which is your reasonable service." Romans 12:1

To follow Jesus is to take up our cross and be crucified. But the sacrifice is the appetites of the flesh. That is what dies so the new nature can live and dwell in victory with God…Thus, the calling to be a sacrifice. It is the only way to walk in the Spirit and have true fellowship with the Father.

Fragile Flower Red

As a flower in earthen sod,
I bloom for thee, oh God.
To blossom with the turn of spring;
To be to you, a beautiful thing.

I lift my Fragile Flower Red
Upward from my earthen bed;
To draw light from God above,
Strength and peace and joy and love.

As a flower, I bloom for thee
That passersby may stop and see.
Your fragrance and beauty I am,
Flowered in grace as a man.

As a flower in earthen sod,
I bloom for thee, oh God.
Upward, I lift my head,
As a Fragile Flower Red.

"Be not conformed to this world, but be ye transformed, by the renewing of your mind, that ye may prove what is that good and acceptable and perfect will of God."

When we look to God as our source, we blossom, much like a flower that draws light from the sun. When we blossom, like a flower, we display the glory and beauty of our creator to all who care to stop and look. This is our divine providence.

From Tears To Smiles

They attack from every side.
Zing!! Go their arrows of pride.
Like demons up from the pit of hell,
They come to laugh at those who fell.

They care not how hard you've tried.
They're here to kill God's love inside.
But though insults come our way,
We'll still find peace most every day.

God is greater than all their dares.
The Holy Spirit proves God cares.
When we're faced with many trials,
God will replace our tears with smiles.

"And God shall wipe away all tears from their eyes" Revelation 7:17

The time is coming and even now is when God will wipe away every tear, replacing it with a smile because we are the redeemed and have followed Him into Glory, laying down our own lives to be His children.

Almighty God

The Lord, our God is Almighty,
Full of power and might.
He is all-powerful, all the time.
Ready for battle, day or night.

There is no power
Greater that His authority.
There is no other kingdom
Able to last an eternity.

God is greater that anything;
That was or is or will ever be.
He is the Lord of lords
The King of kings, God Almighty.

"And when Abram was ninety years old and nine, the Lord appeared unto Abram and said unto him, I am the Almighty God, walk before me and be thou perfect." Genesis 17:1

Almighty God means endued with power, so much power that there is no other greater than His. Almighty is to be full of might. Able to create, destroy, build, and tear down or to do anything that is or is not possible. There is no end to His power. His power is so great that He can call forth something into existence from nothing. Imaging what it can do for you.

Our Time of Prayer

Oh child of God,
Why do you despair?
My angel's camp
Is around you everywhere.

You may not see
My guiding hand,
Yet I am with you
And I understand.

You are troubled
About so many things.
Your eyes see nothing
Of what my will brings.

Be of good courage
And walk in the light.
Stand up for the truth,
In the power of my might.

For I love you dearly
And will always be there.
Go now my child
Until our next time of prayer.

"Let not your heart be troubled; ye believe in God, believe also in me" John 14:1

We are troubled on so many sides; we fret about everything, yet God is there, waiting to care for us and be God in our lives. Isn't it about time to listen to Him and rest in His love?

Male And Female

God took the rib of man
To make a helpmeet for life.
His new creation was female
And she became his wife.

This, in the beginning act of God,
Was a male and female thing.
There was no same sex union,
But only male and female to sing.

A godly union of two,
No longer one alone.
Both joined in God's love,
To form a Godly home.

"And the Lord said, it is not good that the man should be alone; I will make an helpmeet for him." Genesis 2: 18

Isn't it great that God made man's helpmeet as a woman? There was no male for male or female for female unions like today. God, in the beginning, did it right. Man is the one, in his wickedness, that distorts it and gets confused.

There Is Still Time

Inspired by God's love,
I pen this rhyme.
For you, dear friend
While there is still time.

Hear my words
For they are true.
Jesus, God's only Son
Gave His life for you.

A ransomed soul
On the cross of Calvary.
As a penalty for sin
That you might go free.

Call upon Jesus
To give you life anew.
His grace and power
Will see you through.

God patiently awaits
Your humble cry.
Salvation is your
To accept or deny.

"For God so loved the world that he gave his only begotten Son; that whosoever believeth in him should not perish, but have everlasting life" John 3:16

God has done His part. Now it is up to us. Salvation is ours to have and to hold or to reject and deny. We are the "Whosoever's" of this world and it is up to us to believe in Him. I chose life. What about you?

Thy Soul To Keep

Open your eyes oh world of lust.
Hear the cries and woes of the just.
Oh harlot of this endless night,
Prepare for your approaching plight.

And to the tyrants of this world,
Who rape the earth and steal her pearl.
You who deny the living God,
Shall be cut down by His might rod.

And to you who love His Holy name,
The just, the poor, the meek and the lame.
Be of courage and of good cheer,
For the Lord of Host is very near.

To those who die alone
And wander through life without a home,
And to the children who suffer and weep,
Their soul shall the living God keep.

"The heathen raged, the kingdoms were moved; He uttered His voice the earth melted" Psalms 45:6

God is in the midst of His people to avenge those who would destroy His work of grace. His voice melts the earth and all its evil. But we, the children of God, go on to maturity being exercised in godliness.

With Eagle Wings

I mounted up with "Eagle Wings"
To soar above the clouds.
I viewed life above its trials,
Separate from the crowds.

Just me and God, together in the day,
His love to behold.
With "Eagle Wings", He led the way,
My future to unfold.

Forgiveness and peace in a distance,
Suddenly I could see.
Joy and happiness trailed behind,
Then overshadowed me.

With "Eagle Wings" I soared above
Life's every trial.
Now I walk by word of faith,
Rejoicing with every mile.

"They that wait upon the Lord shall renew their strength; they shall mount up with wings as eagles; they shall run and not be weary; and they shall walk and not faint" Isaiah 40: 31

It is the power of God that causes us to overcome the flesh and the evil of this world. We can walk in the Spirit, Soar above the clouds and dwell in the joy of our salvation. This is our heritage from the Lord.

The Caveman's Prayer

Lord! I cannot see the light of day,
For this cave is dark and yet I pray.
Life has overwhelmed me on every side,
Because of oppression, fear and pride.

But You, oh Lord, are my strength.
My refuge in times of worry and fear.
You will deliver me from all of this,
And will gently draw my soul near.

I will yet stand victorious,
Even though I am in a cave.
Before I can see it happen,
I give You, Lord, all the praise.

For the light of day will come
And I will still give You praise,
For helping me through it all,
When I prayed in the cave.

"I cried unto the Lord with my voice; with my voice unto the Lord, did I make my supplication; I poured out my complaint before Him; I showed before Him my trouble" Psalm 142: 1 & 2

It's o.k. to cry before the Lord and to complain about the injustice in our lives. But the truth of real faith is to also declare the victory, acknowledging the power of God and His willingness to act in our behalf.

For The Joy Set Before Him

I could have lived forever
As a simple mortal man.
I could have called 10,000 angels
To help me to stand.

But I laid down my life
Despising the shame.
For the joy set before me
Was your life to gain.

I could have stayed in heaven
As the supreme ruler of all things.
I could have played among the stars And listened for the flutter of angel's wings.

But I laid down my life,
Despising the shame.
For the joy set before me
Was to know you by name.

I could have sent my armies
To rid the world of sin.
I could have destroyed the earth
As I did way back when.

But I bore the suffering of the cross, Despising the shame.
For the joy set before me
Was to take away your pain.

I could have done a lot of things
To make this world right.
Or I could have done nothing
And ignored you plight.

But God so loved the world
That I endured the shame.
For the joy set before me
Was your love to gain.

"Looking unto Jesus, the author and finisher of our faith; who for the joy that was set before Him endured the cross, despising the shame; and is set down at the right hand of the throne of God" Hebrews 12:2

We are the joy that was set before Jesus and the sole reason for Him to endure the shame of the cross; so we could know Him. Imagine that!

A Glorious Church

A glorious church
Awaits the return of the Lord.
One without spot or wrinkle,
Whose hearts have been restored.

Still of a fallen nature,
Yet led by Spirit's call,
Walking towards the light,
Knowing they'll never fall.

Some weary from the battle
And others just entering the fight.
Some strong in the Lord
And some newborn by His light.

A glorious church
Awaits the Lord's return.
Battered, bruised and torn,
Yet fighting evil at every turn.

"But we are come unto mount Sion; and unto the city of the living God, the heavenly Jerusalem, and to an innumerable company of angels; To the general assembly and church of the firstborn, which are written in heaven and to God, the Judge of all; and to the spirits of just men made perfect" Hebrews 12:22 & 23

The Lord will return for a glorious church; those whose spirits are just and their lives on the road to maturity. We are that glorious church. What a destiny.

Godliness

Godliness comes from God
Through patience and lots of time.
It's like a heavenly wind over a troubled sea,
As our Lord prepares in us, His life Divine.

He pulls in currents deep,
Reaching into our very soul.
While His Spirit takes by force,
Every storm & billow's roll.

Together, in hidden concert,
Our Lord brings new life and more.
Working with our free will,
To put holiness where sin was before.

So when God's holy wind
Rushes into our everyday pace,
Let His overwhelming Love,
Form a sea of eternal grace.

For God's will is to be holy
And we must participate.
He does the work from within
As we pray, repent, and wait.

"But refuse profane and old wives fables and exercise thyself rather unto godliness; for bodily exercise profits little: but godliness is profitable unto all things, having promise of the life that now is, and of that which is to come" I Timothy 4:7&8

We are encouraged by the scriptures to be Godly to actually exercise ourselves in the practice of holiness. This is pleasing unto the Lord and beneficial to us in both this life and the one to come.

His Call To Glory

Jesus said, "Take up you cross
And follow after me."
His call to Glory,
Is to reject Satan's plea.

We are to lay down our lives,
Even unto the death,
That He may raise us up again
To live with Him in Holiness.

The way up to Glory,
Is the way down in life.
To take up our cross,
Is to avoid anger and strife.

Death to the old man,
Fallen to the nature of sin.
Chosen by the Lord,
To be "Born Again".

So take up your own cross
And follow after Him.
Deny your fallen fleshly nature
And be free from all that sin.

"And they overcame him by the blood of the Lamb and by the word of their testimony, and they loved not their lives unto the death." Revelation 12:11

Our call to glory is to defeat the enemy of God. It is our joy to be bought by and bathed in the blood of Christ. However, it is our testimony and the fact that we are willing to lay down our own lives, for the sake of the kingdom of God, that gives us power over the enemies of God. This is true victory.

Stewards of Grace

As we have received the gift from God,
We are to manage it to profit all.
As good stewards of His grace,
We now can rejoice and stand tall.

God wants us to flow in His Spirit,
With gifts manifested to heal and bless.
He seeks those who will share His grace,
So others can also find God's very best.

We are the stewards of His glorious grace,
The ones He chose to put in charge.
We are they that will ultimately decide,
The grace that is given, small or large.

So be good stewards before the Lord
And withhold not God's manifold grace.
Do not exclude a soul on this earth,
For we will account to Him, face to face.

"As every man has received the gift, even so minister the same, one to another, as good stewards of the manifold grace of God." I Peter 4:10

God has given us His manifold grace so we can be a blessing to one another. We must demonstrate that unmerited favor in honor and respect for God.

Neglected Gifts

We are encouraged to use the gifts
That were deposited in us by Him.
To neglect them and their operation
Is to fall into disobedience and sin.

They are given to every saint
For the edification of us all.
That's why we have them
And why we obey His call.

Do not neglect the gift inside of you
For someone needs it desperately.
And God has chosen you to be there
With what is needed to set them free.

Do Not Neglect The Gift

"Neglect not the gift that is in thee, which was given thee by prophecy, with the laying on of the hands of the presbytery." I Timothy 4:14

Whether you received the gift by the laying on of hands, prophecy or in the quietness of prayer, it is vital that you acknowledge it, stir it up, and use it to the glory of God and the edification of the church. *Do not neglect it.*

He is Coming Again

The Lord is coming soon, they say.
But no one knows the hour or day.
It is said, He'll descend through a cloud,
With the shout of an angel, clear and loud.

Jesus will come for the "Born Again,"
Who are free from the power of sin.
Those who wait for that blessed day,
Looking for Jesus to come their way.

He will return in the power of His might.
But for many, He'll be as a thief in the night.
While some watch and even pray,
Others will continue to go astray.

But for those who do not sleep,
Who lovingly sow and gently reap.
God has granted His peace of mind,
To keep them until the appointed time

"For the Lord Himself shall descend from heaven with a shout, with the voice of the archangel; and with the trump of God" (Full story, all of chapter five)

The greatest Biblical truth is the literal return of Jesus to this earth and the fact that He is coming for us, His saints. This in itself brings great comfort and joy.

Between Heaven And You

I am sorry you're down today;
It is not easy to walk My way.
There are trials on every side,
Even darkness where Satan hides.

But that's no reason to be blue;
Your Heavenly Father still loves you.
He sees the burden you now bear;
I have made Him keenly aware.

I stand between heaven and you
To insure you make it through.
I will send My love your way,
So be at peace – watch and pray!

God is on your every side;
He alone will turn the tide.
And what now makes you blue,
Will suddenly depart from you.

"My little children, these things I write unto you, that ye sin not; and if any man sin, we have an advocate with the Father, Jesus Christ, the righteous" I John 2:1

Knowing that Jesus has positioned Himself between Heaven and you is of great comfort because He can intercede on your behalf. Where we fail, He did not and this is the basis of our forgiveness. What a plan!

The "I Don't Know Scenario"

Here is the "I Don't Know" scenario.
I hope you will understand.
Because the future and everything else,
Is not really at our command.

Will it rain today?
I don't Know.
Will I live to be 100?
I don't know.

Will my bills get paid on time?
I don't know.
Life is full of "I Don't Knows",
Far too many for me.

There's a lot that "I Don't Know",
About this life and Eternity.
So I'll leave things up to God
Who knows what will & will not be.

He will guide me by His Spirit,
Through life's Thick and Thin.
My times are in His Hands.
He is my only true friend.

"For we walk by faith and not by sight"
II Corinthians 5:2

What an adventure, not knowing what tomorrow will bring, yet believing that our faith in Jesus and His Word will make the way known. When we trust in God for the things we can not know or even perceive, He send us His Holy Spirit to guide us through everything and show us what is to come.

Except Ye Repent

Except ye repent,
Said Jesus, in that day.
You all will surely perish,
And your life will pass away.

That's not a happy word
For those that do evil.
They want their own way
To do their own will.

But Jesus said, nevertheless,
That without a repentant heart,
We shall surely die the death,
Banished, separated, and apart.

"I tell you, nay; but, except ye repent, ye shall all likewise perish." Luke 13:3

The message is clear. Repent or perish. What shall it be?

Taste of Death

Jesus was made a little lower than angels,
So He could suffer the anguish of death.
He tasted death for every man,
Praying for others with His last breath.

He was crowned with glory and honor,
Esteemed, Lord of lords, in every land.
Because, by the grace of God,
He tasted death for every man.

Thus we call Him Savior
For all that He has done.
We know when death befalls us
His sacrifice is our battle won.

"But we see Jesus, who was made a little lower than the angels for the suffering of death, crowned with glory and honor; that he, by the grace of God, should taste death for every man." Hebrews 2:9

Jesus tasted death for every man. That means no human being was left out. He did it as a demonstration of the grace of God, to show God's unmerited favor on mankind. This is why we call Him Savior and worship Him.

True Worship

We are to worship God
In Spirit and in truth.
God desires this of us.

That means we do not
Follow after the flesh,
For it is full of lust.

True worship is to seek
The Lord's love and grace
And to walk in His Spirit.

To finish the course
And to run the race,
With faith to live it.

"God is a Spirit and they that worship him, worship him in spirit and in truth." John 4:24

We must be in the spirit to truly worship God and we must be following the truth of God's word to sustain any real worship experience.

The Power of Praise

There is **POWER** in praise
To keep from going astray.
It's the expression of love
For those who kneel to pray.

There is **POWER** in praise
To walk where angels trod.
It's the expression of joy
For those who know our God.

There is **POWER** in praise
To overcome every trial.
It's the expression of hope
For Satan's every wile.

There is **POWER** in praise
To take depression away.
It is our victory cry
For the trials of everyday.

"Praise waits for thee, O Lord in Sion; and unto thee shall the vow be preformed" Psalm 65:1

God inhabits the praises of His people, Psalms 22:3. We are to call forth His praises, showing the world what great things He has done for us. I Peter 2:9 When we do this, we obtain power to overcome any obstacle.

Blind Leaders

Be careful who you allow to lead you
In all the thing of the Lord.
Some are not really as wise as you think
And you will not be restored.

The blind do lead the blind, you know,
So Jesus said one long ago day.
So leave them alone, as He said
And go on about your way.

Both shall fall into the ditch
While thinking they are right.
But you are not to get involved
With those that dwell in the night.

Blind leaders lead blind people
Down the road to destruction.
So stay away from all of them
Or you will fall into their corruption.

"Let them alone: They be blind leaders of the blind, and if the blind lead the blind, both shall fall into the ditch." Mathew 15:14

Beware of those who teach you. Be sure that they are anointed of God, versed in the authority of the Bible, and full of the Holy Ghost. Remember, blind leaders lead the blind, not those that see. If you see, do not say you don't and walk out of any church or Bible study where a blind leader is teaching. They exist and they are out there waiting to snare you into their false doctrines.

Little Children

Children should obey
Their parents in everything.
This is right before the Lord.

To love mom and dad
And obey them
Is of great reward.

God honors those children who
In humility, strive to understand,
That parents are to lead the way.

God loves all the children,
Grown up or little to be.
Here what the Bible has to say.

"Children, obey your parents in the Lord, for this is right."
Ephesians 6:1

It is right for children to obey their parents, in the Lord. But not mandatory for those parents who are not in the Lord. Parents in the Lord will edify or build up. Those not in the Lord could abuse destroy the little ones God so loves.

Prayer

Prayer is spoken words
Uttered to God above.
Either by voice aloud
Or through a mind of love.

Request for daily help
In life's every affair.
A plea for more power
To overcome Satan's snare.

A time to openly share
Every concern of life.
Things that bring joy
And yes, even strife.

God hears every single voice
That calls to Him in prayer.
He knows their plight
And every burden they bare.

So call upon the Lord
And never ever depart.
And He will answer you
In quietness of heart.

"Be careful for nothing, but in every thing, by prayer and supplication and thanksgiving, let your request be made know unto God" Philippians 4:6,

Prayer is our communication to God. It is where we talk to Him and He talks to us. It is a two-way channel in which we fellowship through the Spirit with our Heavenly Father and the Lord Jesus Christ. What a privilege to know Him and the power of His resurrection.

Judging Secrets

I've got a secret. How about you?
We all have secrets that only we know.
It's a secret because I do not tell you.
But one day our secrets will openly flow.

God will judge them by Jesus,
To see our heart's intent.
He will reveal our inner thoughts,
Until His examination is content.

It does not pay to hide a thing
For in the end, it will come to light.
The Lord will cause all to see,
Our secrets hidden in the night.

So keep a secret or two,
But know that when it's all through,
That God is there to judge
And He will make of it a big to do.

"In the days when God shall judge the secrets of men by Jesus Christ, according to my gospel." Romans 2:16

Judging secrets by the gospel is what God does. He makes sure that nothing is hidden. All will come to light. With that in mind, I would say that our secrets should be our good works. The Lord will have a lot of fun revealing them in that day.

Our Intercessor

He is our Intercessor
Before the throne of God.
His voice is always heard
Before God's judgment rod.

He knows our hearts
With all our frailty.
He hears our prayers
Even from eternity.

Who better could we have
To make our eternal plea?
Than Jesus, the Christ,
Who took our place at Calvary

"My little children, these things I write unto you, that ye sin not; and if any man sin, we have an advocate with the Father, Jesus Christ, the righteous" I John 2:1

Aren't you thankful that we have an intercessor before the throne of God? I sure am. Thank you Jesus.

Time Is Running Out

Time is running out
For all who dwell on earth.
End-time events will hasten
Yet slowly...like a woman giving birth.

Joy and peace shall flee away
Before the mighty hand of God.
Sorrow and terror will prevail
As the Almighty's judgment rod.

Who will survive this time
Destined to befall mankind?
Who will be able to escape
The punishment for their crime?

He who is washed in the Blood
Will not see God's wrath.
He who is found in the Christ
Will God's death angel pass.

Many there shall surely be
That never hear God's song.
Others will also fall into the Devil's lie, knowing not what really went wrong.

But those who have ears to hear
Shall surely sense God's voice inside. They will mount up with eagle's wings and fly away in one glorious ride.

Time is shorter than ever before,
So please...do not delay.
Fall down on your knees,
Repent, read the Bible and pray.

Then be of good cheer and rejoice, for you now bear His name. He is coming to cleanse the earth of all sorrow, sickness, and pain.

"Then cometh the end, when He shall have delivered up the kingdom to God, even the Father, when He shall have put down all rule and all authority and power" I Corinthians 15:24

The time is at hand. We are closer than ever before to that final beat of the clock and that last move of God on the earth. Let us be ready and wanting for the hour so we are not taken by surprise.

An Offering For Sin

It pleased the Lord to make Jesus
An offering for our sin.
For the joy of redeeming us
God chose to sacrifice Him.

He was bruised and beaten
And offered on a cross of despair.
He was ridiculed and cursed
While no one seemed to care.

But it pleased the Lord,
To put Him to grief and misery.
To make Him an offering for sin
So we could walk away free.

"Yet it pleased the Lord to bruise him: he hath put him to grief: when thou shalt make his soul an offering for sin, he shall see his seed, he shall prolong his days, and the pleasure of the Lord shall prosper in his hand." Isaiah 53: 10

It pleased the Lord to make Jesus' soul an offering for sin. It was the only way to bring us back to Him. He was and will always be the Lamb of God, slain for the sins of the world. He was the sacrifice that keeps us clean from the penalty of sin and full of God's grace.

A Gift From The God of Eternity

They traveled by light of shining star,
From lands both near and very far.
To see what God had done,
To pay tribute to His Only Son.

Wise men and shepherds and angels too,
Made haste to see this "Big To Do".
Son of God made Son of Man ...
Born of a virgin in Bethlehem.

A little child in a far away land,
Known in eternity as "The Great I AM",
Came to show us a more excellent way,
To live life in abundance every day.

Wrapped in simple swaddling clothes,
From holy head to tiny toes
And placed in a manger's stall
Though He be Lord of all.

The Word of God in human flesh,
Given to all by Spirit's breath.
They called Him, "JESUS of Galilee",
A gift from the God of eternity.

"Now when Jesus was born in Bethlehem of Judea in the days of Herod the king, behold, there came wise men from the east to Jerusalem, saying, where is that is born king of the Jews?" Mathew 2:1-2

The apostle John tells us, in chapter three, verse 16 that Jesus was indeed a gift from God. He so loved the world that He gave His only Son. How great is that? What a wonderful gift.

Thank You Heavenly Father

Thank you Heavenly Father
For this beautiful day
And for the many blessings
That come our way.

For by your Spirit
Comes joy untold,
As hearts are mended
And lives made whole.

Thank you Heavenly Father
For this beautiful day.
It is with deep appreciation
That we kneel to pray.

For Jesus, our Lord
Has set us free
And given us eyes of love
To behold your majesty.

"This is the day which the Lord hath made; we shall rejoice and be glad in it" Psalm 118:24

Even the day is blessed of God. He keeps us on track and leads us into His will that we night be to the praise of His glory.

God's Little Tree

If I were a tree, to fills the sky,
For all to see and wonder why.
I'd shade the world on a hot summer's day
And beckon to all who pass my way.

I'd offer a branch to a feathered friend
And grant a kiss to the howling wind.
I'd sway in a gentle evening breeze
And change the seasons with falling leaves.

I'd be there, come rain or shine,
Down through the ages, till the end of time.
And I'd stand tall for all to see,
Because I am God's little tree.

"The righteous shall flourish like a palm tree; he shall grow like a cedar in Lebanon. Those that be planted in the house of the Lord shall flourish in the courts of our God. They shall still bring forth fruit in old age; they shall be fat and flourishing to show that the Lord is upright. He is my rock and there is no unrighteousness in Him." Psalm 92:12-15

We who are planted in the house of the Lord do indeed flourish and bear His fruit of love, peace, joy, longsuffering, kindness, faith, self-control, meekness and all the other attributes of His Holy Spirit. This is our destiny.

Baptism of Water

John the Baptist said that he indeed
Baptized with water unto repentance.
A symbol of a converted heart,
Immersed in water symbolizing a new start.

Our baptism is a portrait of death
And yet also a symbol of new life.
It reminds us that we are dead to sin
And alive to all that is pure and right.

We were raised from a watery grave,
To serve the Lord on this earth.
This is the reason for our baptism
And why God gave us a new birth.

"John did baptize in the wilderness and preach the baptism of repentance for the remission of sins. I have baptized you with water but he shall baptize you with the Holy Ghost." Mark 1:4 & 8

Baptism in water is essential but not a requirement for salvation. It depicts what happened inside of us, true repentance, and seals the experience in a vivid picture of death, burial, and resurrection. It is the best way to identify with the passion of Christ.

Galilee, OH Galilee

Galilee, Oh Galilee,
He walked your shores that day,
Telling stories of God's kingdom
And helping those who went astray.

Galilee, Oh Galilee,
He sailed upon your seas
And walked on your waters,
For all to watch and see.

Galilee, Oh Galilee,
How I wish I were there,
To have seen Jesus
With all His love and care.

Galilee, Oh Galilee,
Where storms quickly blow
And where our Savior walked
One day so long ago.

"And He began again to teach by the seaside; and there was gathered unto Him a great multitude; so that He entered into a ship and sat in the sea; and the whole multitude was by the sea on the land" Mark 4:1

What a joy it must have been to be there, in the crowd, when Jesus walked along the seashore and taught the multitudes. Imagine being in Galilee with Jesus and His disciples as they drew the crowds. It must have been an experience of a lifetime.

Baptism In The Holy Ghost

I went through the standard "Water Baptism"
And was also baptized into the body of Christ,
By the power of the Spirit of the living God,
But still needed something in my day-to-day life.

Then I heard of another baptism
That would give me power and set me free.
The baptism in the Holy Spirit,
Offered to all who want to walk in victory.

I believed but had no power to overcome.
I trusted but still could not see God's hand,
Until I realized that I could receive this baptism,
Just like all the others, by faith in the Son of Man.

So I received the Holy Spirit into my life
And went on by faith to do His will,
Baptized in the Spirit, His gifts to flow
And my humble and needy heart to fill.

"And when Paul laid his hands upon them, the Holy Ghost can upon them; and they spoke with tongues and prophesied." Acts 10:6

The baptism in the Holy Ghost is different than other baptisms because it opens a channel through which the gifts of God operate. The 12 men spoken of first received John's baptism, which was of repentance and faith in a future savior, yet to come. However, when they heard that Jesus was that future messiah, they believed on Him and went through water baptism. This is the standard salvation experience. It wasn't until Paul laid his hands on them that they received the gift of the Spirit and knew the fullness of this baptism.

The Bread And The Stone

The Tempter said these words,
"If thou be the Son of God,
Turn this stone into bread"

But Jesus, our Savior,
Knowing He was being tempted,
Said these words instead;

"It is written: Man shall not live
By bread alone; but by every word,
That proceeds out of the mouth of God."

God speaks to every soul
That we might know the difference
Between what is right and wrong.

Listen! And you will hear His voice,
That you may do His will,
And find the place where you belong.

"And when the tempter came to Him, he said, If thou be the Son of God, command these stones be made bread" Mathew 4: 3

It seems that the tempter comes to us at the weakest point in our faith and journey. It is there that we stand or fall, as though we were in a valley of decision. However, if we, like Jesus, use the Word of God, it will give us strength and dispel any confusion.

He is Risen

He is risen
And lives forever more.
He has conquered death,
Passing through its door.

He is risen
Bodily from the grave.
He is alive.
Our debt's been paid.

He is risen
As Lord in my life.
He is my deliverer
From sorrow and strife.

He is risen
And is alive for sure.
Jesus is Lord,
Now and forever more.

"He is not here, He has risen. Come, see the place where the Lord lay" Mathew 28:6

We serve a risen Savior who is alive, not a dead prophet. He lives and is seated at the right hand of the throne of God to ever make intercession for the saints. Praise God, Jesus is alive. He is risen from the dead.

The Wrath of God

The wrath of God shall come
Upon those who choose not to see.
God will sit in the heavens
And laugh at their calamity.

He will not protect the defiant,
Those who reject His destiny.
He turns them over to be reprobate,
Because they chose their own reality.

He will bring their mischief
Upon their own foolish heads.
They will reap what they sow
For that is what God said.

There is no escape from an angry God,
Whose love is scorned to follow after sin.
He will surely avenge His righteous name,
And pour out His wrath upon all of them.

"He shall sit in the heavens and laugh: the Lord shall have them in derision. Then shall he speak in his wrath, and vex them in his sore displeasure." Psalms 2:4-5

The anger of the Lord is no joke. To fear Him is the beginning of wisdom. He is an awesome God, full of power and might. He is a great God, ready for battle. He is our Savior and friend, but woe unto those that hate Him or reject His mercy to follow after evil. They are the heathen, who will only know the wrath of God.

Easter Is

Easter Is...
When sadness turns into joy.
And time seemed to stand still,
As we remember Golgotha's hill.

Easter Is....
When darkness gives way to light,
And demons have to flee,
As the Son of God enters our reality.

Easter Is...
When we are buried in baptism,
As a symbol of death to sin,
And to rise up again to serve Him.

Easter Is...
When we die to inward lusts.
And His life is born anew,
Replacing the old with someone new.

Easter Is...
When God and man are one again.
As His Spirit and ours unite,
In fellowship, in love and all that is right.

Easter Is....
When our hearts rejoice
In the only begotten Son
And live in the victory He has won.

"And they crucified Him, and parted His garments, casting lots: that it might be fulfilled that was spoken by the prophets. " Mathew 27:35

Easter is not about bunnies and colored eggs. It is about the Salvation of our souls and the resurrection of Christ in us. Has Easter happened to you?

Rock of Ages

Rock of Ages, draw me nigh,
To a place that is higher than I.
Where peace and safety surely dwell,
Far from the torment of an endless hell.

I stand in awe, Lord, of Thee,
Knowing that this is where I can be.
To hide in cover of gracious wing,
Makes my heart to laugh and sing.

My lips are full of wonderful praise.
My heart and hands I humbly raise,
To Jesus, God's ageless Rock.
I come, Lord, while others mock.

O' Rock of Ages, draw me nigh
To a place that is higher than I,
That I may dwell in perfect peace.
O' Lord, what sweet release!

"Hear my cry, o Lord, attend unto my prayer; from the end of the earth, I will cry unto thee, when my heart is overwhelmed: lead me to a rock that is higher than I" Psalm 61: 1-2

Jesus is the, "Rock of Ages" and He is that Rock that is higher than all of mankind. He is to whom we cry when overwhelmed and to whom we praise when all is well.

Baptism of Fire

They asked of Jesus
To sit at His side in Glory.
But they did not understand,
This is that incredible story.

For the baptism that Jesus faced
Was one of fire through suffering.
His destiny led Him to the cross,
And this baptism was for a King.

Baptized by suffering for the glory of God
Is to endure the fire that befalls your life.
But knowing that it is not destructive to ruin,
Rather purifying to manifest Holy light.

"And they said unto him, Grant us that we may sit, one on thy right hand, and the other on thy left hand, in glory. But Jesus said unto them, Ye know not what ye ask: can ye drink of the cup that I drink of? And be baptized with the baptism that I am baptized with?" Mark 10: 37-38

The baptism that Jesus was baptized with was one of suffering. He was the suffering servant. He did this for us, that we might not suffer but have an abundant life here on this earth. Nevertheless, this baptism is also upon certain others that God chooses to do His divine will. The question is, can you be baptized with this same fire? If not, do not seek it. You will know if it is part of God's call upon you.

No Other Name

There's no brilliant light
Of heaven's newest star.
Only a compelling hope,
For healing life's every scar.

There are no camels,
Or deserts, windy and cold.
Only God's great love,
And salvation to unfold.

There are no shepherds
To herald His matchless worth.
Only this truth self-evident,
That He came to give "New Birth."

There is no salvation
In any other name,
Only in Jesus Christ,
His love to claim.

There is no other
Pathway to heaven's throne,
No other name given,
Than His name alone.

"Neither is there salvation in any other: for there is none other name under heaven given among men, whereby we must be saved" Acts 4:12

Jesus is the only name that saves us from our sin and sets us free from the bondage of Satan. He alone is the way to God's love and favor. (Read John 3:16)

Help From Above

The Lord has not left us
All alone to wander through life.
He has begun a good work in us
So we can be free from strife.

He will perform that good work
Every day, until we are fine.
Working in us to do His perfect will,
Until He returns to redeem the time.

So we wait for help from above,
Knowing the Lord's return is near.
Being confident in everything,
We do indeed always persevere.

"Being confident of this very thing, that he that has begun a work in you, will perform it until the day of Jesus Christ." Philippians 1:6

We are not left alone to figure things out, when it comes to our faith and walk with God. We should take comfort in the fact that there is a work of grace going on inside us, originated by God, Himself and He will not abandon it. He will continue to perform it until the day when Jesus returns. Knowing this encourages us to keep at it and never give up.

The Lord knows

The Lord knows
The difficulties we face.
That's why He gives us
His marvelous grace.

He does not wonder
What to do and when.
His awesome and mighty power
Is available to all that follow Him.

Storms will come and go
As Satan plays his dirty tricks.
But we can calm the raging seas
If our hearts are truly fixed.

A little faith in action,
To declare the Word of God,
Will lift us up to new heights,
To walk where angels trod.

Hope and trust will lead us
Along life's every day,
As we follow after Jesus
Ever listening to obey.

"For even hereunto were ye called: because Christ also suffered for us, leaving us an example, that ye should follow His steps."
 I Peter 2:21

The Lord knows all about us, our strengths, weaknesses, desires, concerns and fears. No matter what we go through, He knows and is willing to deliver us, as we follow after Him in obedience.

God Is Faithful

God is faithful
Even when we are not.
He watches over His Word,
Crossing T's and dotting dots.

He is a very present help
In times of sorrow and pain.
We can trust in His Word
For sunshine and latter rain.

He alone holds our future
In the palms of His hands.
He leads us as a loving Shepherd
Into green pasture lands.

God is faithful
To always understand.
Though He is Lord of all,
He is our greatest fan.

"Let us hold fast the profession of our faith without wavering; for He is faithful that promised." Hebrews 10:23

God has always honored His Word and commitments to man. He sends His word out of his mouth and it always accomplishes what He sent it to do. He is faithful.

See O' Man

See, oh man, the trees.
They sway in heaven's breeze.
Some with ripened fruit,
Others barren to the root.

See, oh man, the apple tree,
With the only fruit to see.
No oranges, figs or tangerine,
Only the apple, pure and clean.

See, oh man; look with your heart,
At the fruit both sweet and tart.
Both life here and all eternity,
Await the fruit from your tree.

Time grows short till harvest comes.
When the fruits of life are all but done.
See, oh man, what will you ever do?
For one day, God will ask fruit of you.

"Can a fig tree, my brethren, bear olive berries?, either a vine figs? So can no fountain yield both salt water and fresh. Who is a wise man and endued with knowledge among you? Let him show out of a good conversation his works with meekness and wisdom."
James 3:12-13

It is our choice to flow with salt or fresh water. We are called to walk in the Spirit and bear Godly fruit, not fleshly deeds.

Ask Me Now

Hello my child.
How are you today?
I waited for your call
And have much to say.

A word in due season
To cause your faith to soar.
A morsel of truth
To quiet the lions roar.

So hear, my beloved,
Before you go on life's way.
Receive a special blessing
By what I have to say.

It's not by might or by power,
That you should gain success.
But by my Holy Spirit,
That brings you life's very best.

Ask me now, my child
For all that you need.
For I bless everyone
Who's willing to believe.

"A man hath joy by the answer of his mouth; and a word spoken in due season, how sweet it is" Proverbs 15:23

It is the Word of God that is spoken to us at just the right time that keeps us and teaches us how to be in this world. We too should pay close attention to the words we speak that they may be a word in due season for someone else.

At The Cross

I looked at the heavens
And saw your face.
But, at the cross
I found your grace.

I searched the world
For joy each day.
But, at the cross,
I learned to pray.

I was confused
And went astray.
But, at the cross
I found my way.

"But God forbid that I should glory, save in the cross of out Lord Jesus Christ, by whom the world is crucified unto to me, and I unto the world" Galatians 6:14

May we always be mindful of the cross and its affect on our lives. It is the symbol of salvation and the instrument of purification.

Consider The Clock

Consider the clock
That ticks away the time,
Second by second as
You read this rhyme.

Listen at the passing
Of this beautiful day.
Observe how fast
Our lives pass away.

Today becomes tomorrow
When yesterday is done.
Dreams and aspirations
Become memories undone.

Both joy and sorrow
Pass through our day,
As though a child
Had come to play.

There's plenty of time
To do our own thing.
For in these moments
Life proudly sings.

But in the day
And this very hour,
We live our lives
As a fragile flower.

Faster and faster
The time passes away,
As we boldly march
Through life's array.

Finally to stop,
As does our times,
To listen as Judgment
Sounds its awful chimes.

"And I saw a great white throne, and Him that sat on it, from whose face the earth and the heaven fled away, and there was found no place for them. And I saw the dead, small and great, stand before God; and the books were opened, and another book was opened, which was the book of life; and the dead were judged out of those things which were written in the books, according to there works" Revelation 20:11-12

It is high time to pay attention to our deeds, our attitudes and the way we live this life. Why? Because one day, we will stand before the throne of God and give an account.

Two Become One

Jesus said that man
Should leave mother and father,
To join with his wife,
So they could become one flesh.

It was because, from the beginning,
He made them, male and female.
Becoming "One Flesh" together,
Is life's greatest joy over all the rest.

No man should try to destroy,
What God has joined together.
For it is ordained by God,
And no one can make it better.

"Have ye not read, that he which made them at the beginning made them male and female, and said, for this cause shall a man leave father and mother, and shall cleave to his wife: and they twain, shall be one flesh? Wherefore they are no more twain but one flesh. What therefore God has joined together, let no man put asunder." Mathew 19: 4-6

In the beginning, God chose a man and a woman to join together into one flesh. This, of course, is a portrait of Christ and His church. They two, separate and alone, now become one in thought, union of soul and spirit. This is the intimacy that God desires with all of His children.

Forgiveness

If you cannot forgive
Those who offend you,
How can God forgive,
When you make Him blue?

Forgiveness offers freedom
To the repentant soul.
It opens God's heart
To forgive and make you whole.

God does not honor
The unrepentant heart.
Instead, He closes up heaven
And keeps Himself apart.

So forgive those
Who have offended you
And God will be there,
To forgive and bless you.

"Be ye therefore merciful as your Father is also merciful. Judge not and ye shall not be judged, condemn not and ye shall not be condemned: forgive and ye shall be forgiven" Luke 6:36-37

Forgiveness is a command of the scriptures. Jesus taught the concept, during His earthly ministry. It is a blessed thing to forgive because it allows God to be the Judge and act on your behalf in the face of the transgressor.

Mercy Endures Forever

We ought to be praising God
Every hour of every day.
Why? Because of His mercy.
It does not end or ever fray.

His unmerited favor
Will last for eternity.
You cannot stop it
Or cause it not to be.

His mercy endures forever
And it's freely given to us,
That we may praise Him
And flee from sinful lust.

So bless the Lord, all who sin
And repent to serve the Lord.
For His mercy will not ever fail
And you will surely be restored.

"Praise ye the Lord, give thanks unto the Lord: for he is good: for his mercy endured forever." Psalm 106:1

We should continually give thanks and praise the Lord for being merciful towards us. Why? Because we do not deserve it, yet He gives it to us that we may come to know Him.

We Must Endure

We must endure unto the end,
That's what Jesus said.
Persecution will surely come,
But love will rule instead.

We must endure with grace,
All the trials of this life.
We must put away our anger
And overcome sorrow and strife.

For he that endures to the end,
Has run the course of faith.
He can rest assured of salvation,
When he enters heaven's gates.

"And ye shall be hated of all men for my name's sake; but he that endures to the end shall be saved." Mathew 10:22

No matter what we face in life, we are to follow Jesus. If we are hated for doing so, so be it. Our purpose in this life is to be like Him and to spread the good news of His gospel. This, at times, will take endurance and faith. We must never give up.

Gifts For All

God will give to some, the call.
Gifts to each, not one too small.
For one must speak, while others pray,
That all may know God's Holy way.

Apostles, Prophets, and Teachers of men,
All chosen to war against Satan and sin.
Wisdom, Knowledge and Interpretations too,
Are given by the Spirit to see us through.

One gift for you and another for me,
That we may join to set men free.
Many gifts given to every soul,
Yet one body, made pure and whole.

Gifts of God, received by faith,
To all who seek His face and wait.
That Jesus may be exalted on high,
And deliver us from Satan's lie.

"Now there are diversities of gifts, but the same Spirit. And there are differences of administrations, but the same Lord. And there are diversities of operations but it is the same God, which works all in all." I Corinthians 12:4-6

The Holy Spirit gives us the gifts; God the Father sees to their operation and our Lord Jesus overseas their administration. All work together to make sure we have the necessary gifts to accomplish that to which we have been called.

Tongues of Hell's Fire

The tongue is a little member of the body.
It can speak truth that edifies to inspire,
Or be ablaze with angry words,
Straight from hell's tormenting fire.

Always destructive and full of hate,
Ablaze with jealousy, pride and lust.
This is the tongue that knows not God
And speaks from a lack of faith and trust.

Let not this tongue be yours to wag
And be not like those that always do.
Both good and evil can flow off the tongue.
Allow only the good to come from you.

"And the tongue is a fire, a world of iniquity: so is the tongue among our members, that it defiles the whole body, and sets on fire the course of nature; and it is set on fire of hell." James 3:6

We can bless or curse with the tongue. We can express love or hate. The point is, our choice can either set us on fire from hell or love from heaven. What we say does make a difference and is noticed by God, as to its origin, every idle word.

Holy Spirit

Holy Spirit, Lord divine
Send your love and make it mine.
Come Lord Jesus, for all to see.
Holy Spirit, breathe on me.

Holy Spirit, Lord divine
Fill my heart with new wine.
Come Lord Jesus, hear my plea.
Holy Spirit, breathe on me.

Holy Spirit, Lord divine
Bring me joy and peace of mild.
Come Lord Jesus, set me free.
Holy Spirit, breathe on me.

Holy Spirit, Lord divine
Be my Lord, all the time.
Come Lord Jesus, Your life to see.
Holy Spirit, breathe on me.

Holy Spirit, breathe on me.
Lord of glory, I come to Thee.
Holy Spirit, breathe on me.
Come, Lord Jesus and Comfort me.

"God is a Spirit; and they that worship Him, must worship Him in Spirit and truth." John 4:24

May we always sense the presence of the Lord through His Holy Spirit. It is that sweet Spirit that beings us joy, peace and fullness of life. His very breath brings power, enlightenment and love.

Obedience To Christ

We do not war against flesh and blood,
For they are just like us in this life.
We fight against evil spirits and impure thoughts,
That attack our minds that are not right.

But if we challenge the thoughts
Putting them on immediate trial,
We can examine which are of God
And which need to be tossed in a pile.

Bringing every high thought into
The obedience of Jesus Christ, our lord,
By holding it up to the knowledge of God,
Is how our hearts and lives are restored.

So when you are confused and troubled,
Lost as to what to do next in your day,
Apply the Word to every single situation,
And cast down imaginations in your way.

"For the weapons of our warfare are not carnal, but mighty, through God to the pulling down of strongholds, casting down imaginations and every high thing that exhausts itself above the knowledge of God and bringing into captivity every thought to the obedience of Christ;" II Corinthians 10: 4-5

If we know the knowledge of God, which is His word, we can put every thought on trial, measuring it against the application of the gospel. Every thought that sets itself up above that knowledge must be cast down and brought into the obedience of Christ. This is to apply scripture, denying the fleshly sins and walking in the Spirit.

I Surrender All

I surrender all to Thee,
My love, my life and liberty.
For if I should rule life's throne,
You Lord, would stand alone.

But with my will I offer Thee,
My love, my life and destiny.
That you should rule this throne.
So I'll never again stand alone.

I'd surrender all I have to Thee,
For but a glimpse of your majesty.
That I may live within your perfect love,
Both here on earth and in heaven above.

"Trust in the Lord with all your heart, and lean not unto your own understanding; in all thy ways acknowledge Him and He shall direct thy paths" Proverbs 3:5-6

Surrendering to God is the first step towards finding your way in life. When we surrender, we trust and obey and then and only then does the path become clear.

Is That All There Is?

Is that all there is?
Says everyone these days.
Because life has lost its luster,
Holding no joy of triumphant praise.

Is there no more to life
Than just getting by?
Is that all there is,
But to stop and reason why?

Come, let us ponder
Matters pursuant to the soul.
Things that make us happy
And dreams grown old.

If that is all there is,
It could be a deceptive web.
A snare that's designed,
To cloud what God has said.

Or heaven's window,
Closed by disobedience.
An unwillingness to follow
Good old common sense.

That's all there is,
Because no faith exist.
Only an acceptance,
Of that which persist.

But God is greater
Than what now is.
He always responds
To faith that lives.

"Now faith is the substance of things hoped for; the evidence of things not seen" Hebrews 11:1

When we see with the eyes of faith, we see all that is or could ever be. This is the essence of living faith.

I Will Remember

Death has come.
It has fallen upon you.
But I will remember,
That you may live anew.

As part of me,
You will live again,
Cherished in my heart,
As a dearest friend.

Where you are,
I now cannot be,
Until I am summoned,
By the God of eternity.

But until that day,
When I enter death's door,
My eyes will behold you,
At peace on the other shore.

"Jesus said unto her, I am the resurrection and the life; he that believeth on me, though he were dead, yet shall he live And whosoever lives and believeth on me, shall never die" John 11:25-26

We remember loved ones and somehow keep them alive. But real life is only found in a steadfast belief in Jesus.

Portrait of the Dammed

They seek after peace of mind
But make choices that
Do not rhyme.

They are giants made of sand
That fall apart when
It's time to stand.

They hear words of faith
But turn a deaf ear
Until it's just too late.

They seek after reasons why
But reject the truth
To believe Satan's lie.

They believe that all is well
But travel a road that
Leads straight to Hell.

"But as the days of Noe were, so shall also the coming of the Son of man be. For as in the days before the flood, they were eating and drinking, marring and giving in marriage, until the day that Noe entered the ark; and new not until the flood came and took them all away; so also the coming of the Son of man be" Matthew 24:37-39

This is a vivid picture of the damned. They didn't have a clue until it was too late. Beware that the light in you is not really darkness. We do not want to be counted among the damned.

Rejoice With Me

Oh child of God
Why do you cry for Me?
It was my joy
To go to Calvary.

Through My pain,
You were healed.
In My suffering,
Your fate was sealed.

Oh child of God
Do not cry for Me.
I came from heaven
To set you free.

For you, My child
Death has no sting,
Because you made Me
Your Lord and King.

Oh child of God
Rejoice with Me,
For your name
Is written in eternity.

"O death, where is thy sting? O grave, where is thy victory? The sting of death is sin, and the strength of sin is the law. But thanks be to God, which gives us the victory, through our Lord, Jesus Christ." I Corinthians 15:56-57

Jesus paid it all, living the life we could not live because of sin and dying the death we should have died because of sin. His righteousness became ours, giving us freedom and victory over death and hell. That's Grace!

Heaven Is His Throne

Heaven is the throne of God
And the earth is His footstool.
Where is the house of His rest?
And His kingdom to rule?

His presence is everywhere
And no places are without Him.
He created all things for Himself,
Even the battle so He could win.

Yet there is a house built of flesh,
A kingdom to rule, a human heart.
That God should be all in all
And we would no longer be apart.

"Thus sayeth the Lord, heaven is my throne, and the earth is my footstool; where is the house that ye build unto me? And where is the place of my rest?" Isaiah 66:1

The throne of God is in heaven yet Jesus said to pray that it would be here on earth as it was in heaven. That is now happening every time a human heart is converted and Jesus becomes Lord. He rules the earth through our flesh.

Shout The Victory

Call upon the Lord.
He will not turn you away.
His wonderful grace
Is meant for every day.

Reach out to Jesus
In your time of need.
He is sure to deliver
If you let Him lead.

Stand up in faith
In all that you do.
Speak not of things
That make you blue.

Be of good courage
In these last days.
Then lift up your hands
In thanksgiving and praise.

Claim your salvation
And shout the victory.
For Jesus, the Christ, has come,
To set you Free! Free! Free!.

"The thief cometh not but for to steal and to kill and to destroy: I am come that they might have life and that they might have it more abundantly." John 10:10

If Jesus said it, it is so. We are supposed to have life abundant. That means rich and full of meaning. It is ours to claim, in accordance to the will of God. It is our destiny.

The Fruit of The Spirit

The fruit of God's Spirit
Is not the same as what we display.
His fruit is full of life and strength.
But man's fruit is full of decay.

The Spirit manifests love, joy, peace
And lots more that is good.
But the flesh is not so inclined,
To manifest life like it should.

Idolatry, witchcraft, hatred,
And all that sort of evil stuff,
Is all that man has in him,
Without God's heavenly tough.

It's love against hate
And kindness against anger.
It's peace against wrath
And goodness against murder.

The flesh must die for the Spirit to live.
That is how we tell which fruit is.
All is subject to our command.
We choose our fruit or His.

"And they that are Christ's have crucified the flesh with the affections and lust." Galatians 5:24

We are encourages to walk in the Spirit. That means to allow His fruit to be manifested in you. That is to be full of joy, love, peace, kindness, faith, longsuffering, and all the rest of the attributes of God. To see Jesus in you is to see these manifestations of fruit. Think about it.

Stand Up Tall

When you're trodden down and blue
And stuck, not knowing what to do,
It's hard to walk upright
When Satan wants to fight.

Though God has won the victory,
We often still sit in pain and misery.
But this one thing I surely know,
God loves me and won't let me go.

So have faith in His finished work.
He will deal with devils that lurk.
No more will they dominate you.
The Holy Spirit will see you through.

Be of Good Cheer and Stand Up Tall!
Hear God's voice and answer His call.
For this is the glory and the power,
As Jesus dwells in you, hour by hour.

"Stand therefore, having your loins girt about with truth, and having on the breastplate of righteousness." Ephesians 6:14

We are called to faith and expected to stand in our faith before the enemies of God. We have His armor and His Spirit. What more do we need?

With Open Arms

He waits, oh man, with open arms.
By Holy Spirit, He woos and charms.
Calling by name, thy sins to right,
Pleading, in love, for thee tonight.

Hear, oh man, His urgent request
For time has few moments left.
Man, with all his deeds of crime,
Shall suddenly fall, in God's time.

He waits, oh man, for you to say,
"Lord, forgive me, I'll now obey."
With open arms, He calls your name,
To join others who share His fame.

Come, oh man and find your way
For God, through Jesus, holds the day.
Make Him Lord and you will find
Love and Joy and Peace of Mind.

"If we confess our sins, He is faithful and just to forgive us our sins, and to cleanse us from all unrighteousness" I John 1:9

The Lord waits for us to make that decision. He cannot and will not forgive until we confess to Him our trespasses. That means we will live out a life of guilt and regret until we call upon the Lord. Then and only then does He cleanse us from the past and all its hurts.

Grace Defined

We are saved by grace,
Which is unmerited favor.
It is God's love towards us,
Without all the hard labor.

Grace is a gift from God,
Given to all who believe.
It is offered to all men,
But blesses all who receive.

Faith is the Godly key,
To unlock its marvelous work.
Grace is what gives us hope,
And shows us what we are worth.

"For by grace are ye saved, through faith and that not of yourselves: It is a gift of God." Ephesians 2:8

Saved by grace, a gift of God. Get the point? You exercise faith in Jesus and God gives you unmerited favor. What a deal.

Healing And Confession

Jesus wants us well,
Body, soul and spirit.
That's what the scripture says,
But Satan doesn't want us to hear it.

Confess our faults, it says,
One to another in love.
This is a sure fire way,
To receive healing from above.

Because the effectual fervent prayers
Of the righteous saints of the day,
Will reach up to God in heaven,
And return with power to make a way.

"Confess your faults one to another, and pray for one another, that ye may be healed. The effectual fervent prayer of a righteous man avails much." James 5:16

The body of Christ desperately needs healing, one saint by one saint. It needs cleansing from immorality, backbiting and a host of other sins of the flesh. When we pray for one another and confess our faults, we open up a new channel of blessings by which we can be healed.

The Glory of His Majesty

Earthen vessels have never shown,
Such glory that once was known.
Through time and all of eternity,
Came the glory of His Majesty.

Full of love and full of grace,
He dwelt among the human race.
To heal the sick, the blind and lame,
To free mankind from sin and shame.

With earthen vessel He conquered all,
By perfect obedience to His call.
For this we praise His Holy name,
Full of grace and full of fame.

The glory of His Majesty,
Still shines through from eternity.
Again and again to meet life's call,
In earthen vessel, to conquer all.

"For God who commanded the light to shine out of darkness, hath shined in our hearts, to give the light of the knowledge of the glory of God in the face of Jesus Christ. But we have this treasure in earthen vessels, that the excellency of the power may be of God and not of ourselves." II Corinthians 4:6-7

God became man in the body of Jesus, the Christ. He was totally God and totally man, in one place and at one time. But the story didn't end there. Now, through His Holy Spirit, He lives again on the earth in us, another earthen vessel to conquer all.

The Masters Love

In the quiet of the hour,
I walk with my Lord each day.
Sometimes in prayerful thought,
Of what the Master is about to say.

Oft times I sit in silence,
Gazing into heavens door,
Wondering why it was,
That He chose me to adore.

My grace could never compare
With the beauty of the tree.
Why even the flowers
Are greater in stature than me.

Yet He watches over me
With tender loving care.
As a father loves his child,
My Lord is always there.

I listen for His voice,
As His presence draws near.
Knowing that the Masters' love
Will wipe away every tear.

"We love Him because He first loved us" I John 4:19

God is Love. His very existence is the essence of love. He so loved the world that He gave us Jesus to save us from our sins. What manner of love is this? It is the great and powerful love of God. Isn't it wonderful?

After Grace

The wrath of God will take away
All wicked and evil men.
They who spread immorality
And follow after sin.

Life as we know it will end,
Giving way to a new society.
There will be a new heaven and earth
To replace the one that used to be.

And God will wipe away
Every single sorrowful tear.
He will bless humble hearts
And there will be no more fear.

The Lord will dwell with us
In the city of His grace.
We will worship Him there,
This time, face to face.

"And I saw a new heaven and a new earth; for the first heaven and the first earth were passes away; and there was no more sea. And I John, saw the holy city, new Jerusalem, coming down from God out of heaven, prepared as a bride adorned for her husband. And I heard a great voice out of heaven saying, the tabernacle of God is with men, and he will dwell with them and they shall be his people, and God himself shall be with them, and be their God. And God shall wipe away all tears from their eyes, and there shall be no more death, neither sorrow nor crying, neither shall there be any more pain; for the former things are passed away."
Revelation 21: 1-4

There is no help for the wicked who reject God, but we who seek the Lord and His righteousness have a great future, to know Him and His love.

The Steps Of A Good Man

The steps of a good man
Are ordered of the Lord.
He leads us by still waters
Until our souls are restored.

Our pain and suffering
Is all taken away,
Replaced with great hope,
For a brand new day.

He orders our steps
By Holy Spirit's breath,
That we may overcome
Satan, sin and even death.

The steps of a good man
Are not entirely his own.
They're given by God
So he doesn't walk alone.

"The steps of a good man are ordered by the Lord, and he delights in this way" Psalm 36:23

How great is it to know that God orders our steps? He has called each one of us to a task and has given us a vision or destiny. It is our responsibility to hold on to it, obey it and follow it until it comes into being. Who among you is living out your vision and walking step by step with Jesus?

The Was That Is

Before I came to be, I was
But not as Was Is.
For Was defined, equals before,
But now Is.

So then before I Was,
I must have been.
For God's order of things,
Says, "I AM".

To be in God's order then,
Is to be the Was and the Is.
Waiting to become the Now,
As Was became the Is.

This then, is the "Was That Now Is"
That existed before it was.
It's the perfect will of God
As, "The Was That Now Is".

"I was cast upon thee from my mother's womb; thou art my God from my mother's belly." Psalm 22:10

God knows us even before we come into existence. He knew all of what would be before it came to be and rested on the seventh day from all His works.

Thy Soul To Keep

Open your eyes oh world of lust.
Hear the cries and woes of the just.
Oh harlot of this endless night,
Prepare for your approaching plight.

And to the tyrants of this world,
Who rape the earth and steal her pearl.
You who deny the living God,
Shall be cut down by His might rod.

And to you who love His Holy name,
The just, the poor, the meek and lame.
Be of encourage and of good cheer,
For the Lord of Host is very near.

To those who now die alone
And wander through life without a home;
And to the children who suffer and weep,
Their souls shall the living God keep.

"The Lord redeems the soul of His servants; and none of them that trust in him shall be desolate." Psalm 34:22

The Lord will always watch over His children. Woe unto him that hurts one of these little ones; for God is an avenger of the just and will destroy those who would do harm to His beloved children.

What Manner of Man Is This

What manner of man is this
That calms the wind and sea?
With only a wave of His hand,
He caused my fears to flee.

Who is this mighty man of God
That dares to stand up for me?
With words that echo bold,
He comes from eternity.

He will calm the storms of life
That rain down upon my soul.
He will bear my sorrow and strife
And once again make me whole.

Stormy seas there might be.
But Jesus will show me the way.
His peace will calm my heart
As I kneel to Him and pray.

"And they feared exceedingly and said one to another, what manner of man is this, that even the wind and the sea obey him?" Mark 4:41

Jesus will calm the storms in your life and stop the winds of discouragement and doubt to blow. He is all we need to make it through to the other side of any difficulty.

You're Going To Be Just Fine

Our souls hath He restored.
He who? Of course, the Lord.
With His love and His peace divine,
He said, "You're Going to be Just Fine."

No more sorrow, sickness or pain.
Only His Joy, forever to reign.
As old things slowly pass away,
New things will appear every day.

Be of good courage and patiently wait.
God is never ever too late.
The Lord will see you through.
Why? Because He loves you.

"Wait on the Lord; be of good courage and He shall strengthen your heart; Wait, I say on the lord." Psalm 27:14

There are two kinds of courage, bad and good. Bad courage is courage to do evil. However, good courage is a righteous determination to follow the will of God in your life; to do the right thing.

The Trinity

God is one Lord,
Yet manifest Himself as three.
Father, Son and Holy Spirit,
For all of eternity.

God is a Spirit,
This we should know.
His eternal Fatherhood
Is good to go.

God is Love
Seen in the face of Jesus.
Son of God and Son of Man
Who came to save all of us.

God is seen in a clover.
One clover yet three leafs,
Always seen with three,
Yet only one is our belief.

"And God Said, let us make man in our image, after our likeness." Genesis 1:26a

Who can explain the complexity of God? He is not three Gods. He is one God, a spirit that has chosen to manifest Himself as three eternal modes of existence, being Father, Son, and Holy Spirit. This is no different that one person who is always a father to his children, always a son to his parents and always a spiritual being.

My Guardian Angel

The angel of the Lord
Comes with a mighty army,
To fight the enemies of God.

Then he opens our eyes
That we might see the battle
And walk where angels trod.

Our guardian angels
Beholds the very face of God,
Standing there on our behalf.

Our guardian angels
Are ready with God's power,
To quiet evil's awful wrath.

"Take heed that ye despise not one of these little ones; for I say unto you, That in heaven, there angels do always behold the face of my Father, which is in heaven" Mathew 18:10

We all have guardian angels that watch over us and report back to God. They are ministering spirits especially placed in service to help the saints on their way to glory.

The Perfect Man

The mature man of God
Walks in righteousness.
His life and testimony on earth
Is marked by a Godly rest.

The end of this type of man
Is the ability to walk in peace.
To see through life's annoyances,
To find that sweet release.

Though attacked by Satan
Most every day and on every side,
The perfect man stays in his rest,
Knowing that Jesus will turn the tide.

Faith and trust are real words
That do not fade or easily depart.
For the perfect man is marked
With peace from God in his heart.

"Mark the perfect man and behold the upright: for the end of that man is peace." Psalm 37:37

To be perfect is to be mature in the things of God. Faith, trust, hope and righteousness are not taken lightly because they produce peace that often passes all understanding. This is the mark of the upright. They are at peace, resting in the power of God.

In Seven Days

God created everything
In only six days.
Then He rested on the seventh,
Which left everyone amazed.

What about the trials of life
That befalls all the saints?
What about those great storms
That rage until we faint?

God rested from all His work,
Knowing the beginning from the end.
He made provisions for everything,
Even the souls that fall into sin.

It is a finished work
That we call creation.
When, on the seventh day,
God blessed His work
And all its habitation.

"And God blessed the seventh day, and sanctified it: because that in it He had rested from all His work which God created and made." Genesis 2:3

When God rested from all His work, He did so with the foreknowledge that we would be going through what we are right now. He also made a provision for us so we could believe Him and get through the things that rise up like a storm to destroy us. We now need to labor to enter into His rest and enjoy life, as He wanted us to.

The Angel's Camp

The angel of the Lord
Sets up his camp
Around those that reverence God.

Imagine being there
In the midst of
Where angels trod.

What a joy it is
To know God's protection
And to be in the angel's camp.

It is there that God's children
Are delivered from evil's woe
And led by the Word, heaven's lamp.

"The angel of the Lord encamps round about them that fear Him, and delivers them" Psalm 34:7

Deliverance come through reverence and respect for God and a belief that He will be there with His angels to help you in times of trouble.

Train Up A Child

Train up a child
To do the right thing
And when he or she grows up,
They will cause you to sing.

If values are taught
When the heart is young,
They will last a lifetime
Until the battle is won.

Lifestyle and conscience together
As the voice of righteousness,
Because you trained up your child
With dignity, to be the very best.

So train up your children
In the way that they should go
And they will not depart from it
To follow Satin's promiscuous glow.

"Train up a child, in the way he should go: and when he is old, he will not depart from it" Proverbs 22:6

It is our responsibility to teach values and faith to our children. Failure to do so will result in their destruction at the hand of the enemy. Teaching them what is right saves their souls and shapes their thought process to be good and follow after righteousness.

The Chastisement of The Lord

The chastisement of the Lord
Is what makes us His.
It's the seal of approval
That we are what He is.

What father would not chasten
The children under his care?
What fellowship is there
Unless His image we bear?

If we are not corrected and taught
By the Lord of Host,
We are not sons of God,
Even if that is what we boast.

Every son of the living God
Is under His chastening love.
So open your heart to His leading
And follow Him to your home up above.

"If we endure chastening, God deals with us as sons: for what son is he that the father chasten him not? But if ye be without chastisement, wherefore all are partakers, then are ye bastards, and not sons." Hebrews 12:7-8

The proof is in the experience. If we are the children of God, we will feel His guiding hand, even to the point of correction and discipline. However, let us not confuse God's corrective discipline with His awesome wrath. They are not the same.

As A Man Thinks, So Is He

I am as my thoughts are,
No matter what you say.
If I think good or bad thoughts,
That is what rules my day.

You cannot know me,
As I really am,
Unless I reveal my thoughts,
And become a transparent man.

You are no different than me,
Underneath all the fleshy show.
We all are as we continually think,
Some happy and others full of woe.

So think on the things in life
That brings out the very best.
And you will surely get better
And be able to finally rest.

"Eat thou not the bread of him that hath an evil eye, neither desire his dainty meats: for as he thinks in his heart, so is he: eat and drink, saith he to thee; but his heart is not with thee" Proverbs 23:6-7

Our thinking must surpass those around us that seem friendly but are full of hidden agendas. God wants better things from us.

God's Handiwork

We are the handiwork of God
Created in His very likeness.
He breathed life into us
And gave us His holiness.

Of all the creatures on earth,
Man is the only one like God.
We alone have the capacity
To walk by His staff and rod.

What a mystery this is to see,
How He created the night and day.
Then chose to bless the world
And fashion a man from clay.

"And God said, let us make man, in our image, after our likeness, and let them have dominion over the fish of the sea and the fowl of the air, and over the cattle, and over all the earth, and over every creeping thing that creep upon the earth." Genesis 1:26

No other creature has been blessed like man. We did not evolve from monkeys, nor did we come from the sea. We were created in the image and likeness of God, to have fellowship with Him and to display His character of righteousness in the earth. May we always keep this in mind and offer up our lives to His glory.

Faith or Fear

Faith sustains the soul
In times of crisis or trial.
But fear strips away the future
And steals a joyful smile.

Faith hopes for things to come
And is ready always to believe.
But fear is full of doubt and torment
And enters the heart, only to deceive.

Faith is the substance of things
That is yet to come.
And also the evidence
That what is not will be done.

So which is it for you, my friend
As life overtakes your soul?
A walk in faith, boldly to believe,
Or a life of defeat and a future on hold?

"Now faith is the substance of things hoped for; the evidence of things not seen." Hebrews 11:1

Life is full of choices. We all have them. It's like we are always in a valley of decision and our well-being hangs on the way we think, and how we make choices. I chose to believe God and walk by faith. What about you?

From The Beginning

From the beginning of creation,
Before there were people on the earth.
God pre-determined our destination,
To be like Christ, after our "New Birth."

Through a Godly process
Whereby we are slowly conformed,
We ever grow into the Christ nature
As the world watches with scorn.

Our sin nature to die so Christ may live.
This is the plan for all to trust.
Death to self and the evil flesh
So God can dwell, within us.

Jesus was the first-born
Among many brethren today.
We were Foreknown by our Heavenly Father
And pre-destined to a new and living way.

"For whom he did foreknow, he also did predestinate, to be conformed to the image of his son, that he might be the first born among many brethren." Romans 8:29

God knew ahead of tine who would give their hearts to Jesus and desire to be with God. It is this group of people that he predestinated or pre-determined their destination, to be Christ-like. This is a spiritual reality and is happening in the lives of every born again child of God. The question is, what about you? Are you going through the process or sitting on the sidelines watching with scorn?

Overcoming Fear

Fear is a terrible thing
Because it cripples the soul.
Overcoming it is not easy,
For it spreads and takes hold.

But Jesus said that we who believe,
Should not be easily troubled.
If we believe in God, the Father,
We are to believe in Him, double.

For Jesus is God and the Son of Man.
He rules the heavens and all the earth.
We look to Him for power to overcome
And to transform us through the "New Birth."

We do not have to sit in fear
And let it steal our lives away.
We believe in God's awesome power
And in Jesus, to have victory every day.

"Let not your heart be troubled; ye believe in God, believe also in me." John 14:1

It's high time to push fear out of our vocabulary and life. If God exists, and He does, He is all-powerful. He has also given all authority in heaven and earth to Jesus, our savior. Thus our faith in Him assures us victory over fear and the wilds of the devil.

God Is Love

God Is Love, said Saint John,
So many centuries ago.
He reflected what Jesus said
To contradict evil's woe.

God is Love, not anger or hate.
He doesn't test us with evil.
There is no sinister plot
Hidden in His divine will.

He is a good in every way,
That seeks only the best.
There is no suffering or pain,
Only a call to come and "Rest."

Those who say sickness and sorrow
Comes from a God of Love
Have no understanding of Him
And how He treats His beloved.

"Behold, what manner of love hath the Father bestowed upon us: that we should be called the sons of God: therefore, the world knows not us because it knew not him. I John 3:1 Beloved, let us love one another: for love is of God; and everyone that loves is born of God, and knows God. He that loves not knows not God; for God is Love." I John 4:7-8

All good and perfect things come down from heaven from our Father above. That's all good and perfect things, not evil, sorrow, sickness or any other trial of life. We bring those things to us by bad choices, immorality, disobedience, and acts of the flesh where death reigns. We can rejoice in trials because our loving Father is there to help us out of the problem and to exercise our faith. He does not initiate.

Forgive And Forget

We are asked of our Lord
To forgive and to forget.
Not to harbor trespasses,
But to forgive the debt.

70 X 7 is the magic formula
For us to use in daily life.
490 times in one day
To bring an end to strife.

But the debtor must ask
To be forgiven of the debt.
Because God requires a confession
Before we can forgive and forget.

So if you are a debtor or a forgiver,
Know that God wants love and unity.
That's why He ask us to apologize
And to forgive so both can be free.

"Then came Peter to Him and said, Lord, how oft shall my brother sin against me, and I forgive him? Till seven times? Jesus said unto him, I say unto thee, until seven times: Until seventy times seven." Mathew 18:21-22

Here's the point. Unity is really important among brothers. The trespass, when repented of, should be forgiven, so harmony is kept in place. It is a portrait of God's love and how He deals with us. Do we not come to Him, over and over again, asking for His forgiveness? Many times, it is for the same offence, yet He forgives us. Thus, we ought to forgive others in the same manner.

Before It Happens

Our Lord has a way of knowing
What will happen before it does.
He calls forth the day and night
From that which is and which was.

Today and tomorrow are one,
All to obey His perfect will.
Why even the stars shine,
To give Him a special thrill.

Before it happens in life,
He knows what is our destiny.
That's the majesty of our God,
Who tells us what will come to be.

"For many shall come in my name, saying, I am Christ; and shall deceive many. And ye shall hear of wars and rumors of wars: see that ye be not troubled: all these things must come to pass, but the end is not yet." Mathew 24:5-6

Because He is the Alpha and the Omega, the Beginning and the End, we can trust Him with our future. He knows our destiny and what will enter our day-to-day life. He will also tell us before it happens. We need only to listen.

By His Stripes

Jesus bore our suffering and shame,
On the cross of Calvary.
By His stripes that awful day,
We were given the ability to see.

Thirty-nine strips He bore in His flesh,
One for every disease that is to be.
He suffered that terrible day,
That we could be justified and go free.

How thankful I am that Jesus
Went and carried the old rugged cross.
For by his stripes I am healed
And no more am I counted as lost.

A stripe for cancer, 38 more to go.
Another for Parkinson's, and more.
On and on He bore our shame,
Until salvation was finally restored.

"Who his own self bare our in his own body on the tree, that we being dead to sins, should live unto righteousness; by his stripes, we are healed." I Peter 2:24

Healing is in the salvation process that Jesus secured for us. His suffering and death frees us from sin and heals us from its manifestations. It is by His strips that we are indeed healed.

To Be Holy

My righteousness is as filthy rags
And there is no holiness in me.
While I was lost and dead in sin,
Jesus died on the cross of Calvary.

By His righteousness in life,
I obtained true holiness.
He never once sinned as a man.
Knowing this is to finally rest.

It is God that justifies man
By the blood of His only Son.
It is Jesus that paid the price
And it is how our battle is won.

"For I am the Lord that brings you up out of the land of Egypt, to be your God: ye shall therefore be holy, for I am holy" Leviticus 11:45

We serve a holy God that is full of love and righteousness. He requires the same character in us. Through Jesus and His blood, we can be holy as God is holy.

Holy Conversation

Saint Peter said we should be holy
In all manner of conversation.
There should be a love for others
Without any thought or reservation.

To be and speak holy to all men
Is the call of God for every saint.
For God has called us in love
To do what is good and not to faint.

When others see Jesus in us,
They see His nature and life.
There is joy and hope and love,
And there is no sorrow or strife.

"But as he which has called you is holy, so be ye holy in all manner of conversation:" I Peter 1:15

We are called to be holy. That means to do the right thing and reject evil. When applied to our conversation, it says that our lifestyle is to be without reproach.

The Comforter

He is the comforter;
The one who comes along side.
He is God, the Holy Spirit,
That puts the life of God inside.

When we are down and out,
Feeling all sad and blue,
It is the Holy Spirit of God
That helps us to make it through.

Day-By-Day, He is there for us,
To teach us the Godly way.
He freely offers His wisdom
And gives us power over the day.

As He raised Jesus from the grave,
So shall He quicken our mortal flesh
To form the life of Christ inside
And to have victory over sin and death.

"But the comforter, which is the Holy Ghost, whom the Father will send in my name, he shall teach you all things, and bring all things to your remembrance, whatsoever I have said unto you."
John 14: 26

We are not alone, as children of God. He, the Holy Spirit, is always by our side. His wisdom helps us with every challenge and His great power delivers us from the Evil One. All of God's blessings flow through Him.

Take Heed

Take heed that no man deceived you,
For each will try to make you a fool,
If you listen to what they have to say.

Stay focused on the Godly thing,
You know, that vision
God gave you to proudly sing.

Some will say that they are a big deal,
Even that they are the Christ.
But they follow only what you feel.

But take Jesus unto yourself
And know that He is God.
He holds the power over health.

"And Jesus answered and said unto them, take heed that no man deceive you, for many will come in my name' saying, I am Christ and shall deceive many." Mathew 24: 4-5

Many have come with enticing words of man's wisdom but only one, Jesus of Nazareth, came in the power of the Holy Ghost, to set us free. Many have come saying, I am a Christian and deceived many, leading them astray. It's time to know who the Christ is and who His followers really are.

A Mighty God Is He

The Lord is a mighty God,
Ready for the battle against sin.
He is the avenger of the just
And He always makes sure to win.

He is Lord of lords and King of kings,
Mighty in power against all our enemies.
He is the Alpha and the Omega,
Knowing before hand what will be.

What an awesome God we serve,
Mighty in power yet full of love.
Lord and Savior, Jesus, the Christ,
Our heavenly refuge in God above.

"Lift up ye heads, oh ye gates, and be ye lift up, ye everlasting doors; and the King of glory shall come in. Who is this King of glory? The Lord, strong and mighty, the Lord mighty in battle. Psalm 24:7-8

God is mighty in battle. He is up to the task. He never sleeps or forgets. He is a mighty refuge for all who need help and protection against the attacks of evil.

The Sealing Power of God

We were sealed by the Holy Spirit,
Which was promised to us by Jesus.
He fills and anoints all who believe
After they demonstrate trust.

He is the promise of the Father
That the saints would have power.
Supernatural gifts as a blessing
To show His love in this last hour.

Health for sickness and disease
And those in bondage set free.
That's the promise of the Father
Given to every generation to be.

Holy Spirit of promise,
Fill me with power from on high,
That I may know God's love
And keep others from Satan's lie.

"That we should be to the praise and glory, who first trusted in Christ, in whom ye also trusted, after ye heard the word of truth, the gospel of your salvation: in whom also after that ye believed, were sealed with the Holy Spirit of promise." Ephesians 1: 12-13

The power of God, given to us to live out our destiny. This is knowing that we are sealed with the promise of the Father. It is the blessing of God to every believer.

Praise Waits For Thee

Our praises wait for Thee, O God,
Until the battle is won.
We hold our praise to you, O Lord
Until the vow is done.

Knowing the terror of our God
Upon the wicked of our land,
We wait to be delivered,
By the power of His right hand.

Our praises wait upon Thee
That we may fully rejoice,
When the enemies of our God
Have no scornful voice.

Now we trust, believe and obey
All that you tell us to do,
Knowing that our praises will flow,
When your work of grace is through.

"Praise waits for thee, O God, in Zion: and unto thee shall the vow be preformed." Psalms 65: 1

During the trial, we focus on faith, trust, hope and deliverance. Our praises wait for the move of God. But when He arrives on the battlefield and delivers to us the victory, our praises fill the air and our hearts rejoice. What a great day that is.

Propitiation

Jesus was a substitute for mankind.
That is to say, He died on the cross
Instead of you and me.

He paid the ultimate price for sin.
That is to say, His shed blood
Allowed us to go free.

The soul that sins, it shall die.
That is to say, all have sinned
And fall short of God's glory.

He died for all of us, once for all.
That is to say, where Adam failed,
Jesus did not and gained the victory.

Propitiation means, to substitute.
That is to say, His life was sacrificed
So we could attain our destiny.

"And he is the propitiation for our sins: and not for ours only, but also for the sins of the whole world." I John 2:2

Aren't you glad that Jesus died the death that we should have died? Aren't you glad that He lived the righteous life that we should have lived? He is the captain of our salvation and the Lord of our lives because He stepped into our world and became the way for us to find God.

Flourishing

I long to be like a tree
That flourishes year round.
It is the way of God,
To plant us in good ground.

He shows off His trees
To all that look to see.
It is His righteousness
That will bear fruit in me.

Plant us, oh God of reality
In your glorious house today.
We so long to flourish
That others may know the way.

And we shall bring forth fruit
Even through our old age tears.
Because the Lord loved us
In our youth and later years.

"The righteous shall flourish like a palm tree: he shall grow like a cedar in Lebanon. Those that be planted in the house of the Lord shall flourish in the courts of our God. They shall still bring forth fruit in old age; they shall be fat and flourishing: to show that the Lord is upright: he is my rock, and there is no unrighteousness in him." Psalm 92:12-15

Oh that we might be planted in the house of the Lord; that we may one day be flourishing in the courts of our God…All to show forth the righteousness of God and His love for us.

The Best Gift

The Best Gift of all
Is the gift that is most needed.
If healing is the saint's cry,
Tongues will not treat it.

We should pray that God
Will give severally to all.
Through His Holy Spirit
To meet life's every call.

We are to seek the best gifts,
Those that operates out of love.
Always the most needed ones
Will flow from heaven above.

The best gifts in these last days
Are the gifts that bless and not destroy.
The ones that heal, deliver, and edify
Are the gifts that we are to deploy.

Yet without the operation of love
They are as sounding brass to the ear.
And actually distract from the gospel,
Bringing doubt, confusion and fear.

"But covet earnestly the best gifts: and yet show I unto you a more excellent way." I Corinthians 12:31

All gifts should operate out of love. The best gifts are those that do show forth the love of God and meet the cry of the saint and the need at hand.

Growing Pains

Count it all joy, brethren,
When you fall into despair.
This is the only way to know,
That God is really there.

It's one thing to say,
"I believe that God cares."
It's yet another to see
His mighty armies there.

So every time you fall
Into a some sort of trial,
Believe in the Lord, Jesus,
And begin to laugh or smile.

It's only spiritual growing pains
As you learn patience and faith.
Better to grow now in God's grace,
Than to hold back until it's too late.

"My Brethren, count it all joy when you fall into diverse temptations; knowing this, that the trying of your faith works patience." James 1:2

Without the opportunity to exercise faith, which is to believe in God's Word, we will never learn patience and see Him lead us to victory. The trial or temptation is not from God but it is nevertheless a prime opportunity for us to worship God in the midst of the difficulty.

A Way of Escape

God will make a way of escape
So we can overcome temptation.
He will not allow us to fall
Due to a lack of good education.

There are no temptations
That are not common to man.
This means they are of the flesh,
But we can learn how to stand.

We are drawn away from God
Because of our lustful hearts.
But it is our choice to stay strong
Or give up on God and depart.

So deny the deeds of the flesh
When they seek to lead you astray.
Stand strong in the Spirit
And He will show you the way.

"There hath no temptation taken you but such is common to man: but God is faithful, who will not suffer you to be tempted above that ye are able; but will with the temptation also make a way of escape, that ye may be able to bear it." I Corinthians 10:13

It is our choice to fall or stand. Temptation cannot overcome us. We are drawn away first by a lustful heart. God has not allowed any temptation to overpower us. We, on the other hand, give up too easily. It is time to realize that we always have a way to escape the temptation and to look for it.

Be Thankful

Sometimes it's hard to give thanks
When everything is going wrong.
It's like a very loud noise
That drowns out our song.

Nevertheless, God is still God
And He is there, watching over us.
There is no reason to fret
Or violate our Savior's trust.

So enter His gates with praise
And be thankful that He is good.
His truth is to all generations,
Freely given and understood.

His mercy will last forever
And His love is always there.
He is really on our side
So let Him know you care.

"Enter into his gates with thanksgiving and into his courts with praise. Be thankful unto him and bless his name. For the Lord is good; his mercy is everlasting; and his truth endures unto all generations." Psalm 100:4-5

To be thankful unto the Lord is to acknowledge His worth and Lordship over your life. It is being grateful for all the little things He does in our everyday. Add them all up together and you get one big reason to follow Him.

Blood Bought Redemption

It was the Lord that paid the price
With His own blood at Calvary.
He bought our salvation with blood
So we could find our God-given destiny.

His blood was shed for all of us,
For all that claim the human race.
We who now believe on His name,
Enjoy God's love and grace.

It's a blood bought redemption
That Jesus did for humanity.
He made the ultimate sacrifice
So we could live, love and be free.

We are sprinkled with His blood
From head to the tip of every toe.
Jesus offered up Himself for us;
That's because He loves us so.

"In whom we have redemption through his blood, the forgiveness of sins, according to the riches if his grace;" Ephesians 1:7

We hold fast to a blood bought redemption, in which Jesus laid down His own life and shed His own blood on the cross for our salvation and for the forgiveness of our sins. Any other doctrine is of demons and not the true gospel.

Judgment of All Men

God has called all men everywhere to repent
Because He has set in place a Day of Judgment.
Therefore, we ought to seek His love and grace
And His forgiveness before the time is spent.

That day is a divine appointment
In which He will judge the world.
Both the strong and the weak.
Every single boy and every girl.

We know the day is close at hand
Because Jesus was raised from the dead.
He is the supreme ruler over all
And that is what His disciples said.

This is the final judgment
Of the living and the dead.
When time will be no more
And the book of life is read.

"And the time of this ignorance God winked at; but, now commands all men everywhere to repent. Because he hath appointed a day, in the which he will judge the world in righteousness by that man whom he hath ordained; whereof he hath given assurance unto all men, in that He raised him from the dead." Acts 17:30-31

The Day of Judgment is coming. We know that Jesus will judge us in that day. We have two choices: 1.) Ignore it and suffer the consequences later. 2.) Prepare ourselves now by repenting and getting our hearts in line with His will and set our minds to serve Him in this world.

The Fretter

There once was a fretter,
That needed to do better.
Worry! Worry! All the time,
Caught up in fears of all kinds.

What will happen to me
Because of evildoers that cry?
What will the future hold?
I must, above all things, reason why.

Wait, I hear a voice from heaven.
It is the Lord, telling me not to doubt.
Forget the wicked that rage in the night.
Their candle will suddenly be put out.

"Fret not thyself because of evil men, neither be thou envious of the wicked; for there shall be no reward to the evil man; the candle of the wicked shall be put out." Proverbs 24:19-20

To fret is to worry. This is not good. Saints of God should trust in the Lord and keep their eyes on Him. Looking at the wicked in an effort to figure them out is futile because God has assigned them to failure and vows to extinguish their candle of light. We do not want to be numbered with them.

The Folly of Worry

There is a folly to worry
That some saints get all caught up in.
It is to fret over the wicked that prosper
And fashion devices that support sin.

They will not see God,
Nor know His righteous love.
They are set on a course
That leads to hell, not above.

We need not fret because others prosper
While we are still waiting on God.
Our time is soon to come, even at hand,
For us to walk where angels trod.

Worry is all but folly,
Not for the believing one.
We are to trust and obey
Until the battle is won.

"Rest in the Lord and wait patiently on him: fret not thyself because of him who prospers in his way, because of the man that brings wicked devices to pass." Psalm 37:7

Don't get caught up in the folly of worry. It isn't worth the sorrow and pain. Just keep your eyes on Jesus and trust Him through the sunshine and the rain.

The Wrestling Match

We wrestle not with flesh and blood,
For man is not our enemy.
Instead, we fight demons in the spirit
That seek to steal our destiny.

But our weapons are not earthly,
Like tanks, guns or bombs.
Instead, we "Plead The Blood"
And shout our victory songs.

So do not wrestle with humanity
Even though evil is there.
Go after Satan, the real enemy
And strip his kingdom bare.

"For though we walk in the flesh, we do not war after the flesh: for the weapons of our warfare are not carnal but mighty, through God, to the pulling down of strongholds; casting down imaginations and every high thing that exalts itself above the knowledge of God, and bring into captivity, every thought to the obedience of Christ." II Corinthians 10: 3-6

Don't fight with other people. Just go about your own business, counting on God to be the avenger. He is the one that holds all the power and strength. If we fight in the flesh, we can fall to strongholds and demons. But standing up in the Spirit and using the name of Jesus, applying the knowledge of God in the situation and casting down every ungodly imagination, will always lead us to victory.

Oh' The Blood

Oh, the blood of Jesus
That washed away my sin.
What a great blessing
To have God as my friend.

This one thing I know for sure,
That when I confess my sin,
His cleansing blood will flow,
And I can walk again with Him.

Oh, the blood of Jesus,
How great a sacrifice for me.
For it was the blood of the Lamb
That healed my soul and set me free.

"If we confess our sins, he is faithful and just to forgive us our sins and to cleanse us from all unrighteousness." I John 1:9

It is the blood of Jesus that is the cleansing agent in forgiveness, acceptance by God and salvation of the soul. Without His blood, there would be no payment for sin. Saint John, in chapter three,
says that the wages for sin is death. Jesus paid the price so we could go free to serve God, the Father.

When He Sees The Blood

I can hear the wailing
In many of the houses along the street.
There is a strange and powerful presence
That no army can defeat.

It is the "Death Angel" passing through
To bring a plague upon the land.
But God said, "It will not harm you"
Only the 1st born of the Egyptian man.

When He sees the blood
On your lentils and posts,
He will pass over your dwelling,
To a no blood stained post.

The blood will save God's children
From the death of judgment's day.
Truly a foreshadow of the Christ,
Whose blood keeps God's judgment at bay.

"And the blood shall be to you for a token upon the houses where you are, and when I see the blood, I will pass over you, and the plague shall not be upon you to destroy you, when I smite the land of Egypt." Exodus 12:13

When God sees the blood of Jesus, He passes over, not putting the death sentence upon us. It is the blood of Jesus that sets us free and keeps us free.

One God

Hear me, my brethren.
Our God in one Lord.
There is none before Him.
He alone is our reward.

The heavens are not full
With man made gods of lust.
There isn't a council of gods
That often argues till they bust.

We serve the true and living God,
Who is and was and will always be.
He is one Lord, Creator and Father
To all on earth and in eternity.

"Hear, oh Israel, the Lord, our God, is one Lord." Deuteronomy 6:4

God is one Lord. He alone created all things and there are no other gods, not before Him, along side of Him, or after Him. He is Lord over all things.

The Judgment Seat of Christ

We ought not to judge our brother,
Because we shall all stand before Jesus,
At the judgment seat of Christ.

There will be no way out for us
When we appear before the Lord
To answer for all that is in this life.

Jesus will surely ask of us,
Why we did all those things,
To hurt our Christian brothers.

What will we say unto the Lord
As we stand before Him, face to face
And explain how we didn't love one another?

"But why dost thou judge thy brother? Or why dost thou set at naught, thy brother? For we shall all stand before the judgment seat of Christ. So them every one of us shall give account of himself to God." Romans 14: 10 & 12

Standing at the judgment seat of Christ will surely be a hot seat experience, unless we are prayed up, have forgiven all trespasses, and walking in His will. Few of us will attain that level of Christ-likeness. Nevertheless, we ought to be ready.

One Man

It was by one man, Adam,
That the world fell into sin.
He chose to disobey God's word
And lost God's Spirit within.

No more walks with God
Through the garden of God's grace.
No more close up and personal
To walk along and talk, face to face.

One man, Adam, gave up
The very nature of God.
Never again to stroll along
Where angels once trod.

Evil now flows through his blood
Where only righteousness was before.
He gave up the Spirit of life
To open up death's awful door.

But one Man, Jesus, came from God
To seek and to save that which was lost.
The life of God in man, once again,
Because He paid sin's incredible cost.

"Therefore, as by one man, sin entered into the world, and death by sin; and so death passed upon all men, for that all have sinned. For as by one man's disobedience, many were made sinners, so by the obedience of one, many shall be made righteous." Romans 5:12 & 19

Adam fell and lost the Spirit of God inside of him because of his disobedience; But Jesus obeyed, did not fall and restored what Adam lost. All die in Adam because of sin but all who believe in Jesus shall live in Christ because of His righteousness.

The Passing of Death

I fell from God's grace
Never realizing I carried
The fate of the human race.

I wanted to be like God
Knowing good and evil.
Both seemed good to taste.

I quickly found death
Replaced life in my blood
And hope turned into despair.

Then death passed on
Into my offspring's blood
And they too needed repair.

All have now fallen into sin
And sin and death we also know.
But because of Jesus, we will still win.

"All have sinned and come short of the glory of God." Romans 3:23

All have sinned and fallen from grace. That is the Word of God. The wages of sin is death, but there is a gift of eternal life through Jesus. 6:23. It is our choice to believe and receive or reject and neglect. The refusal keeps us on a path to hell. What say ye?

God Said

God said that I should not eat
Of the fruit of that tree.
He said that it was forbidden
And would surely destroy me.

But the "Evil One" said NO,
That it wouldn't hurt me.
That I should know good and evil
To once and for all really be free.

So I believed the lie
And fell from God's grace.
I lost His indwelling presence
And doomed my entire race.

But thanks be to God
For still loving me.
He sent the promised one
So we all could be free.

"And the Lord God commanded the man, saying, of every tree of the garden, thou may freely eat: but of the tree of the knowledge of good and evil, thou shall not eat of it: for in the day that thou eat thereof, thou shall surely die." Genesis 2: 16-17

When God says, especially as a commandment, we should obey. Adam defied God, knowing the consequences, believing that God was not serious about what He said. He believed a lie instead of God. We ought to believe God and call everyone and everything else a liar.

Our Choice

We are free to choose,
What our destiny will be.
God has given us the choice
To decide our own destiny.

He knows the future
For all of humanity.
Both good and evil
To Be or Not To Be.

Even Salvation is for "Whosoever."
But it is not accepted by all.
Those that find God's grace
Are they that hear His loving call.

Free Will is God's gift
To everyone of Adam's race.
We hold the ultimate choice
To accept or deny God's grace.

"I call heaven and earth to record this day against you, that I have set before you life and death, blessing and cursing, therefore choose life, that both thou and thy seed may live." Deuteronomy 30:19

Our destiny is in our hands. No one else can decide for us, unless we allow him or her to do so by giving up the task because of fear or reprisal. Ultimately, we are the one who exercises our own free will to shape the future.

The Invitation

I heard the knocking, knocking, at the door,
But others around me apparently did not.
I listened once and again and then even more,
Realizing that the knocking would not stop.

I looked around me, ever close to see,
Who was knocking, knocking, at my door?
It was the crucified Christ of Calvary,
Speaking to my heart in a quiet roar.

He's standing at your door
With an invitation for to see.
Open the door and let Him in.
What will your decision be?

"Behold, I stand at the door and knock; if any man hear my voice and open the door, I will come in to him and sup with him, and he with me." Revelation 3:20

The invitation is to all who hear His voice, but the choice is ours to open the door and let Jesus in. His invitation is to dine with Him, to be in His presence and to have fellowship. What will your decision be?

Submission

Wives are to be submissive
To their husbands in the Lord.
For he is the glory of her head
And together they will be restored.

It's not a subservient role
That woman plays before man.
It is rather a love relationship
That is in the palm of His hand.

Only the husband, in the Lord
Is worthy of such true love.
For his authority is to edify
As anointing falls from above.

"Wives submit to yourselves unto your own husbands, as unto the Lord." Ephesians 5:22

My dear wife, I respect your love and appreciate your submission to my judgments when I am in the Lord. I also understand that, at times, I will not have sound judgment and not be in the Lord, as I should. Thank you for those times when you speak up, as my helpmeet, and bring my thoughts back in line with the Word of God.

A Husband's Manifesto

A husband is a man called of God
To portray Christ here on earth.
He is the head of his family
As Christ is head of the church.

He is to love his wife
As Christ loves the church.
He is to care for his wife
To insure she finds New Birth.

He is to lay down his life
For the protection of his wife.
That she may be cleansed
And ready for a brand new life.

The husband is the head
As God intended it to be.
He set the husband in authority
So as to watch over the family.

"Husbands, love your wives, even as Christ also loved the church, and gave himself for it." Ephesians 5:25

We men have an awesome responsibility before God. We are to love, to lay down our life for, to edify and bless our wives. What woman would not want to submit herself to such a man as this?

Grace That Justifies

We are justified by His grace
That we should walk with Him.
It is through this gift of grace
That we find freedom from sin.

But our justification is also seen
In our Lord's glorious resurrection.
For He was raised again from the dead
So we could experience "Divine Selection."

Jesus was delivered unto death
For all our offences in the flesh.
So God could freely justify
And save us from eternal death.

"Who was delivered for our offences and was raised again for our justification" Romans 4:25

It is God that justifies, so why do we still try to be justified, in the sight of God, by good works. Receiving God's finished work of grace allows us to rest in Him.

Grace Is Not A Magic Wand

Grace is not a magic wand
That calls forth thing to be.
It is God's perfect love
Given to sinners like me.

The measure of the gift of Christ
Determines His grace to all.
It is given to help us to grow
And to accomplish our Godly call.

God's grace is given to everyone
The saved, the lost, the small and tall.
But only those who truly believe
Can use it to master their destined call.

"But unto every one of us is given grace according to the measure of the gift of Christ." Ephesians 4:7

It is the measure of the gift of Christ that determines the grace that we receive. The greater the gift, the greater the grace. May we all obtain the gift of Christ in abundance that we may dwell in His grace forevermore.

No One Should Perish

God does not want any to perish,
No not one, especially you.
He knows the depth of your sin
And still offers you life brand new.

It is time to come to repentance
Before it is just too late.
In fact, God wants you to finally
Get real and drop the debate.

God is longsuffering and kind.
He is waiting for you today.
Repentance is to turn around
And forsake sin and pray.

No one, especially God
Wants you to go to hell.
All should come to repentance
So He can make them well.

"The Lord is not slack concerning his promise, as some men count slackness; but is longsuffering to us-ward; not willing that any should perish, but that all should come to repentance." II Peter 3:9

God does not want any to perish. He sends no one to hell. If you end up there, it is because you would not repent and rejected God's plan of salvation, His only Son, Jesus Christ.

Tried By Fire

Our faith is tried by fire
That it might by strong.
Only then to God's praise
And glory to endure long.

Faith tried by fire
To last until He appears.
To keep us in His love
Free from all those tears.

The trial of your faith
Is precious in His sight.
For it is the only way
To walk in the light.

"That the trial of your faith, that being much more precious than gold that perishes, though it be tried by fire, night be found unto praise and honor and glory at the appearing of Jesus Christ." I Peter 1:7

It's all about perseverance; to make it through unto the end and to see Jesus at His coming. It is the trail, or exercising of our faith that keeps us strong and determined to keep on keeping on.

Judging Angels

Did you know that we will
Some day judge angels?
That the saints will
Examine the angelic realm?

That's right, you and me
Will rule over the unseen world.
We will not be sitting back
But will take over that helm.

How much more shall we live
In this world today?
Knowing where we will be then
Will help us to trust and obey.

"Know ye not that we shall judge angles? How much more things that pertain to this life." I Corinthians 6:3

If we can not judge the things of this life, how will be do when we are placed over angels, to judge them? This life is a practice ground for that life to come. It's about time to step up to the plate, be responsible and do the will of God.

Worship IS

Worship Is...To enter His gates with thanksgiving
And the Lord's courts with praise.
To make a joyful noise unto God
And serve Him gladly all of your days.

Worship is ...the Lord's mercy,
That of a great and powerful Master.
His truth last forever and forever.
We are the sheep of His pasture.

Worship is... to love the Lord
And to praise Him for all He does.
To sing and dance and rejoice,
Because of His amazing love.

"Make a joyful noise unto the Lord, all ye lands. Serve the Lord with gladness; come before his presence with singing." Psalm 100:1-2

Worship is to love God with all your heart and to know that you are the sheep of his pasture; that He made us for His pleasure and loves to be with us and to shower us with His love.

Husbands And Wives

Every man should have
His own wife so as to
Avoid sinful lust.

God does not want
His married couples
To sin and loose trust.

Instead of abstinence
That leads to sexual immorality,
They are to come together.

Husbands and wives as one
To avoid the sinful lust,
Is the only way to make life better.

"Nevertheless, to avoid fornication, let every man have his own wife, and let every woman have her own husband. Let the husband render unto the wife due benevolence: and likewise also the wife unto the husband. The wife hath not power over her own body, but the husband: and likewise the husband hath not power over his own body, but the wife." I Corinthians 7: 2-4

Sexual union is reserved for marriage and its fulfillment is to prevent sexual sin. Withholding sex is to deprive your mate and could force him or her into adultery.

The Gathering of Saints

The saints gather together
To rehearse the things of God.
They share the joy of the Spirit
And walk where angels trod.

This is the church of the living God,
The believers in the Christ of olden days.
They know the power of a living God
And dance and sing with both hands raised.

These are the saints that walk with God;
That see His hand in their day to day.
This is the church of Jesus Christ
Walking by a new and living way.

"And when they were come, and had gathered the church together, the rehearsed all that God had done with them, and how he had opened the door of faith unto the Gentiles." Acts 14:27

The saints of God rejoice in what He is doing in their lives. They have a life that is active and full of miracles and faith and meaning. If your life is dull and boring with no visible move of God, you should rethink your relationship and get it right.

Obedience Is Better

It is better to obey God
Than to offer up a sacrifice.
That is what the prophet said
So we night know what is right.

Too often we try to follow
The religious rules of the day
And miss the voice of God
Calling us to trust and obey.

It is time to get it right
And keep a clarity of mind.
God wants us to obey His word
And do it all of the time.

"Behold, it is better to obey than sacrifice, and to hearken than the fat of rams." I Samuel 15:22b

We are to trust and obey. This is our part in salvation. He works in us to will and do of His good pleasure but we are to work it out with fear and trembling in act after act of obedience to His calling.

The Broken Body

His body was broken
That we may go free.
He was the sacrifice
For all of humanity.

He was the bread of live
That came down from above.
God's only begotten Son,
A gift of God's eternal love.

Yet He died for the sins of all
On an old rugged cross.
The "Bread" was broken
But the life was never lost.

So we remember His death
Each time we break bread.
We partake in His suffering
And hold fast to what He said.

"For I have received of the Lord that which was delivered to me, which also I deliver unto you, That the Lord Jesus, that same night, in the which he was betrayed, took bread: and when he had given thanks, he brake it and said, take, eat: this is my body, which is broken for you" this do in remembrance of me." I Corinthians 11: 23-24

The old rugged cross was where my savior died for me. His body broken so I could go free. We can never forget so great a sacrifice and we can never forget so great a salvation.

The Cup of Remembrance

I remember the cup
That we all lifted that night.
It was in celebration
Of God's glorious light.

Then He said to one and all,
"This represents my blood."
He would shed it for me
As they nailed Him to a tree.

Yes I remember that cup
For it was poured out for me
And the sins of the whole world
At a place called Mount Calvary.

Then we drank of the cup
So always to remember
His death on the cross
Until He returns in victory.

Yes, I remember

"After the same manner also he took the cup, when he had supped saying, this is the cup of the New Testament in my blood; this do ye as oft as ye drink it, in remembrance of me." I Corinthians 11:25

And we do partake of the cup in remembrance to remember His death, burial, and resurrection. We, who believe, remember our Lord and know that one day we will see Him, face to face. One day we will take of the cup with Him in heaven.

The Unworthy Partaker

The unworthy partaker
Of the Lord's Supper
Is the one who will not
Examine himself for sin.

It is not right to abstain
From the supper of the Lord.
It wasn't created for a few, but all,
For hope and health to be restored.

We are all unworthy to participate.
That's why we examine our hearts.
We seek forgiveness and peace
So we can be healed and be a part.

The unworthy man, at the supper
Is the one that will not get right.
He is the man that hides his sin
And does not walk in the light.

For as oft as ye eat this bread and drink this cup, ye do show the Lord's death till he come; wherefore whosoever shall eat this bread, and drink of this cup of the Lord, unworthily, shall be guilty of the body and blood of the Lord. But let a man examine himself, and so let him eat of the bread and drink of that cup; for he that eats and drinks unworthily, eats and drinks damnation to himself, not discerning the Lord's body. For this cause, many are weak and sickly among you, and many sleep." I Corinthians 11: 26-30

We should never abstain from taking communion. If there is any doubt concerning un-confessed sin, we have the promise of I John 1:9 which says, "If we confess our sins, He is faithful and just, to forgives us our sins, and to cleanse us from all unrighteousness."

It's a matter of going to God and asking to be forgiven so you can be blessed. Failing to do this and still partaking in the supper causes us to become weak and sickly and even die.

Spirit Baptism

We are all baptized into one body
By the Spirit of the living God.
It is He, who places us together
To walk where angels trod.

Many members of that one body
But nevertheless, all united as one.
Baptized by the Spirit of God
To carry on until the work is done.

There is no room for prejudice
Or division over foolish things.
The Spirit baptism made us one
And this is the song we should sing.

"For by one Spirit are we all baptized into one body, whether we be Jews or Gentiles, whether we be bond or free, and have been all made to drink into one Spirit." I Corinthians 12:13

If we are all made to drink of one Spirit, why is there so much division? Could it be because we do not accept one another and are full of pride? Maybe we ought to take another look at our own relationship with Christ and His Body.

A Faithful And Wise Steward

Who is the faithful and wise steward,
That when Jesus returns will find doing?
Is it the man or woman that is lazy
Or the overseer that is always snoozing?

Who is the faithful and wise servant
That uses his or her time to pray?
Is it those that sleep in the night
Or they that are watching every day?

Blessed is the steward that is looking
For the imminent return of his Lord.
He will be blessed above all men
And find his heart and soul restored.

"Be ye therefore ready also; for the Son of man cometh in an hour when ye think not. And the Lord said, who then is that faithful and wise steward, who his Lord shall make ruler over his household, to give them their portion of meet in due season? Blessed is that servant, whom the Lord, when he cometh, shall find so doing." Luke 12:40, 42-43

A faithful and wise steward is the man, woman, boy or girl that believes that Jesus will return to earth and will ask for an account of their use of His talents, time, gifts and authority. This steward will be looking to the heavens for Jesus and managing his goods in a faithful and honest way, until the time comes to present it all to God.

Falling Short

Sin is falling short of God's glory;
To miss the mark of His righteousness
And to exist outside of His Love.

We are all sinners by human birth,
Full of rebellion, hatred and lust,
Empty of the Spirit of God above.

We have earned a wage for this
That fills our very soul.
It is death, separation from God
An endless sorrow to unfold.

Falling short cost us our soul
And all the joys of life.
But thanks be to Jesus, our Savior
Whose blood makes all things right.

"For all have sinned and come short of the glory of God. For the wages of sin is death; but the gift of God is eternal life, through Jesus Christ, our Lord." Romans 3:23 & 6:23

We all fall short of God's glory but He sent Jesus so we could be restored and blessed through the gift of eternal life. No longer do we fall short but attain unto life and liberty through the finished work of Christ.

The Child of Hell

Beware of those that seem to be religious;
That tell you that theirs is the only way.
They could be making you a child of hell
And will surely lead you astray.

You will be twofold, a child of hell
If you listen to what they have to say.
It all sounds so nice and loving
Until you are captured in their way.

Seek the Lord of the Bible
And know that He is on your side.
Do not follow after man's wisdom
Or get caught up in his pride.

The child of hell is religious
Believing they know His call.
But when it comes down to it,
They know nothing at all.

"Woe unto you, scribes and Pharisees, hypocrites! For ye compass sea and land to make proselytes, and when he is made, ye make him twofold more the child of hell than yourselves." Mathew 23:15

It is important who we sit under to receive teaching. If we give away our right to think independently, we will end up twice the child of hell than the one that is teaching us false doctrine. Know them that are learned among you and do not accept everything anybody says, just because they are a pastor or teacher. Search it out for yourself because ultimately, you are accountable to God and can never say it was their fault that you became a child of hell.

A Little Sleep

A Little sleep can lead to poverty
For the soul that labors not.
But to open both eyes wide
Is to find satisfaction and a lot.

Do not love to sleep
If it lingers into the day.
For soon comes the poverty
To steel your faith away.

So set your hands to work
And eat the fruit thereof.
For life is full of suffering
But increase fosters love.

"Love not sleep, lest thou come to poverty; open thine eyes, and thou shalt be satisfied with bread." Proverbs 20:13

Poverty is a spirit that leads a person to be lazy, with no ambition and a low self-esteem. Hard work changes all of that and keeps you feeling good about yourself. Those in poverty are usually unskilled, unmotivated and uncooperative. Education, self-motivation, and lots of prayer to overcome your past are a sure remedy for overcoming poverty.

Life Abundant

God wants us to live in abundance
Without the threat of loss.
That's why Jesus came to earth
So we could become the boss.

The enemy will steal, kill and destroy
But that is not so of our Lord.
He has come to give life
That all things should be restored.

The abundant life for all of us
Through faith and loving grace.
That our souls would prosper
And God would bless our race.

"The thief cometh not, but for to steal, kill and destroy; I have come that they might have life, and that they might have it more abundantly." John 10:10

Isn't it great to know that God wants to bless us and that Jesus really did come to restore us to a prosperous life of joy, peace, hope and even financial security? How great is that?

No Difference

Racial prejudice is wrong,
For it puts down one and elevates another.
When all know in their hearts
That there's no difference in creed or color.

The Jew and the Greek
Are the same to the Lord.
Both, through God's grace
Are forgiven and restored.

But people hold up one
And put down the other,
Like the blacks and whites
That fight over their color.

But we are all one
In the sight of our Lord.
All can know His love
And can be restored.

"For there is no difference between the Jew and the Greek; for the same Lord over all is rich unto all that call upon him." Romans 10:12

Prejudice is wrong. It is not the way of God or part of the teaching of Christ. If you are caught up in being prejudice, you need to repent and ask the Lord to bless you with humility. Your pride is leading you to a fall and the end of that thing will be your destruction. Give it up before it's too late.

The Lion's Roar

Some protest against war
Saying that such things are wrong.
They know not the battle that rages
Or the joy of its victory song.

But Saint Peter calls us into reality
Identifying our enemy and his lot,
So we can overcome his tricks,
And resist his evil sinister plot.

Like a lion with a loud roar
The enemy searches for its prey.
Someone that is unaware
And filled with fear each day.

But we are not afraid
Of the lion's mighty roar.
For Jesus has set us free,
To stand against it and more.

"Be sober, be vigilant; because your adversary, the devil, as a roaring lion, walks about, seeking whom he may devour: whom resist steadfast in the faith, knowing that the same afflictions are accomplished in your brethren that are in the world." I Peter 5:8-9

If you know that the lion will roar; and you also are aware that Jesus defeated him and that he now has no power, you can tell him to shut up and go on about the business of being free.

A Home In The Heavens

We now live in a house of flesh
But God has a building set aside.
A house not made with human hands
But in the heavens where angels abide.

As this earthly tabernacle dissolves,
We have another made of God,
So we can be with Him always
To walk where other saints have trod.

A house in the heavens
Built to last and eternity.
Far above sin and death
Where all of us are free.

"For we know that if our earthly house of this tabernacle were dissolved, we have a building of God, a house not made with hands, eternal in the heavens." II Corinthians 5:1

God has set aside a place for us in heaven, that we might be forever with Him. This is a great thing and worthy of itself for us to praise His name forever.

The Sting of Death

O death, where is your sting?
What has happened to your finality?
Is there no power in your walls?
How is it that I have found liberty?

Your sting, O death, is sin
And I know all about that.
It has followed me from birth
And bites at me like a rat.

But thanks to Jesus, the Christ of old,
Who overcame death and fulfilled the law.
He is my savior and I now live in Him.
O death, the power is gone from your claw.

"O Death, where is thy sting? O grave, where is thy victory? The sting of death is sin and the strength of sin is the law: But thanks be to God which gives us the victory through our Lord Jesus Christ." I Corinthians 15: 55-57

Death has no more finality because Jesus fulfilled its strength, the law. He became the embodiment of the law and removed its sting, which was sin. Thus we look to Him instead of the law and His righteousness becomes ours and we overcome the sting of death. What a plan.

The Father's Glory

Our good works on this earth
Are to our Heavenly Father's glory.
Every time we allow our light to shine,
We tell our Heavenly Father's story.

But our light must shine before men,
Not under a bushel, hidden from sight.
And the praise comes from others,
That see the good and come to its light.

We must shine as the noonday
Full of faith and hope and love.
This is what causes people to praise,
Our Heavenly Father, up above.

"Let your light so shine before men, that they may see your good works, and glorify your Father, which is in heaven." Mathew 5:16

Our light is to shine forth from us as a beacon; like a searchlight, that becomes a guide to those who have lost their way. It is also a light of hope to all who see it because it reminds them of God and His love for them. This is how praise is initiated and how our Father in heaven is glorified.

Thou Shalt Not Kill

The Bible tells us
That we should not take a human life.
Yet it is legal now
To kill our unborn by surgeon's knife.

This is a distorted thought process
That goes against all that is right.
That's why there is lingering torment
For those that do this evil in God's sight.

Some eggs are protected
Because they will become a living thing.
But the human eggs is regarded
As though it were nothing.

How stupid to think of life
As though it were not real.
This is a snare of the devil
Meant to rob, kill and steal.

"Thou Shalt Not Kill" Exodus 20:13

Killing is wrong, especially when it is our own children. How sad that we have been reduced to such foolishness.

Gay Rights

Some call homosexuality being Gay,
So as to remove the stain of sin.
They claim the right to sexual preference,
To change the natural order within.

But God says that this is wrong
And is actually rebellion against Him.
That they choose to go against God
And follow after the lust within.

So God has given them over to a reprobate mind;
To do what is in their own foolish heart.
He knows they will not enter His kingdom
And will die alone, separated and apart.

My heart is saddened by such things.
But I know that God is always right.
No one wants the loss of an eternal life
But they have chosen to reject His light.

"And even as they did not like to retain God in their knowledge, God gave them over to a reprobate mind, to do those things which are not convenient." Romans 1:28

Homosexuality is not a "Gay" thing. It is a SIN thing that destroys the souls of those that participate in it and the society that tolerates it. However, God will forgive even this and will restore any soul that repents, to a productive and meaningful relationship with Him. It's never too late.

Up From The Grave

Up from death and the grave
Came Jesus, from the dead.
He overcame sin and hell
To become the church's head.

Death could not hold Him
Because He is Lord of all.
By the power of the Spirit
He answered life's call.

He lives today for all of us
Because He arose from death.
He lives today for all of us
To bring us Holy Spirit's breath.

Up from the grave, He arose
To conquer death and hell.
He lives! He Lives! He Lives
To keep us from going to hell.

"And he said unto them, be not afraid: Ye seek Jesus of Nazareth, which was crucified: he is risen; he is not here: behold the place where they laid him." Mark 16: 6

We do not look for Jesus in a grave, like Buddha or other famous religious leaders of the past. He was raised from the grave and is alive and well at the right hand of God, the Father to ever make intercession for us.

The Lord Is

The Lord is
The savior of the soul.
By His stripes
We were made whole.

The Lord is
The Beginning and The End.
The Alpha and the Omega,
Our very best friend.

The Lord is
Our refuge when things go wrong.
A shield and a buckler
From Satan's outstretched arm.

The Lord is
God's perfect love indeed.
A very present help
In times of need.

The Lord is
Ruler of eternity.
Our hopes and dreams,
Our life and destiny.

"I am the Alpha and the Omega, the beginning and the end, sayeth the Lord, which is and was and which is to come, the Almighty." Revelation 1:8

The Lord Is. That is the most important thing to know. Nothing else counts. If God is, then all is well and we can rest in His love and power.

Faith

Faith finds the essence of things
Unseen by the naked eye.
It isn't limited by reasoning
Or ever questions why.

Faith is believing what you cannot see
And trusting in the God of eternity.
Blind obedience is not its theme,
Rather an assurance, not yet seen.

Faith walks above the depths of pain
To bless those who proudly proclaim.
It is by faith that we often talk
And by faith we ought to walk.

"Now Faith is the substance of things hoped for, the evidence of things not seen." Hebrews 11:1

We are asked to believe beyond our sight and senses into the realm of the Spirit and on the Word of God. The substance of our faith, being the Word, is also the evidence of that which we believe for, before it materializes. Thus we have confidence in God that He will watch over His word to perform it.

A Mighty Refuge

God is a mighty refuge
For all who face despair.
He alone can give you rest.
His love is always there.

If your dreams are shattered
And you can't find His grace,
Turn again to the Lord, Jesus,
And seek Him, face to face.

He will reshape your dreams
And make them all brand new.
Each one full of God's love
Especially prepared for you.

Jesus is a mighty refuge
For both great and small.
He is the, "Rock of Ages"
To all who heed His call.

"The Lord also will be a refuge for the oppressed, a refuge in times of trouble." Psalm 9:9

A refuge is a safe place where we are protected. It is a haven of rest where the enemy cannot go. It is a hiding place from evil and oppression. Check it out. It is Jesus, our Savior, and the place of our rest.

Not By Bread Alone

The tempter said these words,
"If thou be the Son of God,
Turn this stone into bread?"

But Jesus, our Savior,
Knowing He was tempted,
Said these words, instead;

It is written: "Man shall not live
By bread alone, but by every word
That proceeds out of the mouth of God."

God speaks to every soul
That we might know the difference
Between what is right and wrong.

Listen! And you will hear His voice
That you may do His will, and
Find the place where you belong.

"And when the tempter came to him, he said, if thou be the Son of God, command that these stones be made bread." Mathew 4:3

Temptation is always directed to take us away from our calling, our purpose. It is usually an attempt at getting us to set ourselves above God in some way by exhibiting pride or some other fleshly desire that excludes God and makes us supreme. Avoid it be quoting scripture to the devil and rebuking him.

The Master of The Sea

What manner of man is this
That calms the wind and sea?
With only the wave of His hand
He caused my fears to flee.

He calms the storms of life
That rain down upon my soul.
He bore my sorrows and strife
That I should be made whole.

He is the Master of the sea
Over its storms the rise up to play.
His peace will calm my heart
As I kneel to Him and pray.

Who is this mighty man
That rules the wind and sea?
His name is Jesus, the Christ
Who took my place at Calvary.

"And He arose and rebuked the wind, and said unto the sea, Peace be still. And the wind ceased and there was a great calm." Mark 4:39

Storms are a part of life but Jesus is greater than them all. He brings stability, peace and harmony to the ragging sea in our hearts. All that is necessary is to ask of Him and you will see His power at work.

They Took Me To Jesus

They took me to Jesus,
Four of my closest friends.
I lay on a sick bed
Lost in a feverish wind.

They took me to Jesus
But were hampered by the crowd.
I was so very sick
Near death and a burial shroud.

They took me to Jesus
Climbing onto the roof above.
Then they tore off the tiles
Lowering me into the Master's love.

They took me to Jesus
And He spoke directly to me.
I was bound by sickness
Until He healed my infirmity.

"And when he saw their faith, he said unto him, man, thy sins are forgiven thee. And immediately he rose up before them, and took up that whereon he lay, and departed unto his own house, glorifying God." Luke 5:20 & 25 (Full story 5:17-26)

Sometimes the faith of others heals the sick that are weakened by infirmity. The important thing to remember He is not too busy to help you. Go before His presence and stay there, in faith, until you can walk away healed.

Zaccheous

I wanted to see Jesus,
But could not because of the crowd.
So I climbed up a sycamore tree
As their passing voices grew loud.

High above their heads,
I watched as the master drew near.
He walked towards me,
Until His face drew near.

Then He stopped and looked up to say,
"Zaccheus! Make haste and come down,
For today, I must abide at thy house."
He chose me from all who gathered around.

The crowd murmured because I was a sinner,
Even though I received Jesus as my Lord.
I repented, giving half my goods to the poor.
All obtained wrongly was quickly restored.

The Son of Man came through Jericho
To seek out and save my lost soul.
That day salvation cane to my house
And this son of Abraham was made whole.

"And when Jesus came to the place, he looked up and saw him and said unto him, Zaccheus, make haste and come down; for today I must abide at thy house." Luke 19: 5 (Full story 19:1-10)

When we experience an encounter with the Son of God, it is life changing. You cannot be the same ever again. The experience is too wonderful and so intense that it heals you, cleanses you, and makes you whole again. Being "Born Again" or Saved is to know this first hand.

The Stranger

We walked along the road to Emmaus
Talking about the Christ with a stranger.
Little did I know then
That He was our Lord and Savior

He questioned why we were sad
And inquired as to our talk.
We told Him of the Christ crucified
And those events as we continued to walk.

Then He began to teach us from the scriptures
As we dined together in a strange familiarity.
Our hearts burned inside as He spoke
But in the breaking of bread, we knew it was He.

Then suddenly He was gone
As though never really there.
Only then did we understand
The gospel message He came to share.

"And their eyes were opened and they knew him, and he vanished out of their sight." Luke 24:31 (Full story 24:13-35)

Too many Christians are caught up in the events of their lives that they overlook what is right in front of them. Their eyes are closed by fear, doubt, pride or a host of other things and they cannot see Jesus who is standing in their midst. Don't let that happen to you.

Our Healer

We have an assurance
From God's holy Word.
That He is our Healer.
But this, you've heard.

Pills treat symptoms
That linger forever and a day.
But when Jesus gets involved,
Sickness just goes away.

So call upon the Lord
And trust in His Word.
Be blessed and of good cheer
And obey what you've heard.

God will not forsake you
Or leave you alone to die.
He is the Lord of lords
And to whom we cry.

"For I am the Lord that heals thee" Exodus 15:26b

God knows how to take care of us. We should not be worried about such things. However, He does ask of us to diligently hearken unto His voice and obey Him so He can keep us in His will and blessings. (See the full text of 15:26)

Iniquity Purged

It is God's mercy
That purged our sin.
It is the truth that
Makes us whole again.

He gave mankind favor
When he did not deserve it.
He opened our eyes to see
When we were lost to it.

It was God's mercy and truth
That purged our iniquity.
His unmerited favor came
And set our spirits free.

By mercy and truth, iniquity is purged: and by the fear of the Lord, men depart from evil." Proverbs 16:6

Thank God for His mercy. Without it, we would be forever lost and without hope.

God Will Take Care of Us

The economy goes up and down
Like the ebb and flow of a sea.
But, those who trust in Jesus,
Find peace, joy and stability.

We should not worry
About things to eat or wear.
God will take care of us.
He will always be there.

So when the economy
Ebbs and flows like a sea,
Rest in the Lord
Knowing He will surely see.

"And he said unto his disciples, Therefore I say unto you, take no thought of your life, what ye shall eat, neither for the body, what ye shall put on. The life is more than meat and the body is more than raiment." Luke 12:22-23 (Full story 12:22-34

We can trust in the Lord to go before us, follow after us and lead us to prosperity and blessings. He came that we might have abundant life and will deliver it to all that believe.

A Lamp Unto My Feet

Your Word, oh Lord,
Is a lamp unto my feet.
It illuminates the way ahead
So I will not know defeat.

Your Word, oh Lord,
Is a light unto my path.
It keeps my heart calm,
Free from anger and wrath.

Without it's heavenly glow,
I would be groping in the dark.
Lost as to what to do next
And where to even start.

"Thy word is a lamp unto my feet and a light unto my path." Psalm 119:105

It is the Word of God that lights up our way so we can see the truth and follow it. There is just enough to take the next step but plenty to see the road ahead.

All Paths

All the paths of the our Lord
Are comprised of mercy and truth.
But not all of us walk therein.

Only those who keep
The covenant of the Lord,
Are assured to walk with Him.

Mercy is given to those
Who honor His testimonies
And obey the Lord each day.

This saint will be blessed of God
With all of His mercy and truth
As he walks along life's way.

"All the paths of the Lord are mercy and truth, unto such as keep his covenant and testimonies." Psalm 25:10

Keeping the Lord's covenant and testimonies is the key to finding mercy and knowing truth. We are asked to participate in our own salvation by doing justice and loving mercy. What an honor.

May our Lord bless you and keep you and cause His face to shine upon your life. God bless you in all that you do.

Rev. John Marinelli